The Five C's of Dinosaurs

1. Created by God
2. Cursed by the Fall (sin)
3. Catastrophe (Global Flood)
4. Conflicts with humans
5. Confusion (about dinosaurs)

"For in six days the Lord made the heavens and the earth, the sea, and all that is in them, but he rested on the seventh day."
                    Exodus 20:11

 GENESIS apologetics   www.genesisapologetics.com

HOW DO DINOSAURS FIT INTO THE BIBLE? SCIENTIFIC EVIDENCE THAT DINOSAURS LIVED RECENTLY

Daniel A. Biddle, Ph.D.

Copyright © 2017 by Genesis Apologetics, Inc.
E-mail: staff@genesisapologetics.com

GENESISapologetics

www.genesisapologetics.com
A 501(c)(3) ministry equipping youth pastors, parents, and students with Biblical answers for evolutionary teaching in public schools.

HOW DO DINOSAURS FIT INTO THE BIBLE?
SCIENTIFIC EVIDENCE THAT DINOSAURS LIVED
RECENTLY
by Daniel A. Biddle, Ph.D.
Printed in the United States of America

ISBN-13: 978-1543174250

ISBN-10: 1543174256

Print Version August, 2017

Dedication

To my wife, Jenny, who supports me in this work. To my children Makaela, Alyssa, Matthew, and Amanda, and to your children and your children's children for a hundred generations—this book is for all of you.

We would like to acknowledge Answers in Genesis (*www.answersingenesis.org*), the Institute for Creation Research (*www.icr.org*), and Creation Ministries International (*www.creation.com*). Much of the content herein has been drawn from (and is meant to be in alignment with) these Biblical Creation ministries.

"Guard what has been entrusted to you, avoiding worldly and empty chatter and the opposing arguments of what is falsely called 'knowledge'—which some have professed and thus gone astray from the faith. Grace be with you."
—1 Tim. 6:20–21

"This is the Lord's doing; it is marvelous in our eyes."
—Psalm 118:23

Contents

About the Author

Dr. Daniel A. Biddle is president of Genesis Apologetics, Inc., a 501(c)(3) organization dedicated to equipping youth pastors, parents, and students with Biblical answers for evolutionary teaching in public schools. Daniel has trained thousands of students in Biblical Creation and evolution and is the author of several Creation-related publications. Daniel also serves as the Vice Chairman of the Board of The International Association for Creation, a non-profit ministry serving to unify the Biblical Creation movement. Daniel's experience and qualification in the secular realm includes a Ph.D. in Organizational Psychology from Alliant University in San Francisco, California, an M.A. in Organizational Psychology from Alliant, and a B.S. in Organizational Behavior from the University of San Francisco. Daniel has worked as an expert consultant and/or witness in over 100 state and federal cases in the areas of research methodologies and analysis.

About Genesis Apologetics

Genesis Apologetics is a non-profit 501(c)(3) ministry that equips Christian students and their parents with faith-building materials that reaffirm a Biblical Creation worldview. We are committed to providing Christian families with Biblically- and scientifically-based answers to the evolutionary theory that many children are taught in public schools. Our doctrinal position on Biblical Creation aligns with Answers in Genesis and the Institute for Creation Research (ICR), two of the largest Creation Apologetic Ministries in the U.S.

Readers are encouraged to view our free training resources at *www.debunkevolution.com,* *www.genesisapologetics.com* and our YouTube Channel (Channel Name: Genesis Apologetics).

Introduction

See our Dinosaur Video: *www.genesisapologetics.com/dinosaurs/*

The secular viewpoint on dinosaurs directly opposes what the Bible teaches. In a nutshell, the secular idea is that dinosaurs evolved through death of the unfit and survival of the fittest random mutants starting about 220 million years ago and ending at a supposed extinction event about 65 million years ago. This view invokes the trinity of time, chance, and death as the *creators* of dinosaurs.

But according to biblical history, dinosaurs were intentionally designed by God, each made to reproduce after its own kind, and were spontaneously placed on Earth just thousands of years ago. The following Bible passages outline some dinosaur basics:

1. God created **all living things**. Therefore, God created dinosaurs (Genesis 1; Exodus 20:11; Colossians 1:16; John 1:3).
2. God created all land-dwelling, air-breathing animals on the **6th Day** of Creation, right before He created man (Genesis 1:24–25).
3. Tallying the genealogies in Genesis 1–11, this 6th Day occurred about **6,000 years ago**, so dinosaurs were placed here fully-formed (in several different "kinds") at that time.
4. Adam's first job from God was to name **all** of the animals (including dinosaurs) after they were **all** created (Genesis 2:20).
5. After God created all animals, He gave Adam and Eve the charge of **taking dominion over every living creature**: "Be fruitful and multiply; fill the earth and subdue it; have dominion over the fish of the sea, over the birds of the air, and over **every living thing** that

moves on the earth" (v. 28). All of God's creatures were present when this dominion order was given.

6. The book of Job describes two dinosaur-like creatures: **Leviathan** and **Behemoth**. Behemoth is given the title of God's "chief" or "first in rank" over all God's creative works (Job 40:19). A plain interpretation of the 13 characteristics that describe this animal match a sauropod dinosaur that was "made along with" man (verse 40:15).

7. All land-dwelling, air-breathing animals **died in a worldwide Flood** (except those on Noah's Ark) about 4,400 years ago (Genesis 6:7, 7:20–23). Part of the reason for this worldwide extinction event was that "all flesh" (including animals) had "corrupted their way on the Earth" (Genesis 6:12).

8. Not all animal "kinds" that got off the Ark after the Flood survived for long in the new, post-Flood world (e.g., many dinosaurs). While we don't know the details, many animal kinds (and probably most of the dinosaurs) **quickly went extinct** after the Flood. Some dinosaurs, however, survived for centuries after the Flood, and contributed to the dragon myths and legends that exist all over the world.[1]

Which of these two viewpoints on dinosaurs is correct? Were all varieties of dinosaurs the products of time, chance, and "survival of the fittest" millions of years ago? Or, were they placed here by an intentional, all-powerful God who spoke them into existence, and then later wiped out in the Global Flood described in Genesis?

Next, we'll explore 12 lines of reasoning that provide evidence that the historical view of Genesis is accurate. Rather than dinosaurs being used to "prove" evolution, dinosaur design and the dinosaur fossil record actually fits the "biblical hypothesis" better than the one provided by evolution!

Evidence #1: Clever Design

Some dinosaur design features are just plain astounding. We'll explore these fantastic creatures by focusing on two: Triceratops and Sauropods.

Triceratops

Figure 1. Triceratops[2]

Let's make a reasonable assumption that the two massive horns (up to four feet long) protruding from its skull had a purpose—such as ramming either for defensive purposes or against other triceratops for mating rights.[3] How is it possible to mount a head that weighed a couple thousand pounds that was over eight feet long[4] onto a body that could run over 30 miles-per-hour,[5] and still allow it to turn around every which way? The occipital condyle—that's how! Take a look at the perfectly round ball that's on the bottom of the Triceratops skull in Figure 2.

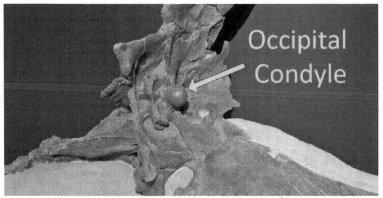

Figure 2. Occipital Condyle[6]

The occipital condyle is a hard, round-shaped bone that protrudes from the base of the skull that mounts to the anterior end of the spine—just like a trailer ball-and-hitch design.

Figure 3. Trailer Hitch[7]

The head of a Triceratops was among the largest of all land animals, with some making up one-third of the entire length of the dinosaur's body. In fact, the largest Triceratops skull ever found has an estimated length of 8.2 feet,[8] indicating it could have weighed thousands of pounds by some estimates. The occipital condyle enables the massive head of the Triceratops to be mounted securely to its body in a way that allows it to rotate while this massive beast rammed its head into other dinosaurs! That takes some engineering!

Where are all the semi-Triceratops fossils with "evolving" occipital condyles? They simply don't exist. When these creatures are found in the fossil record, they all have nicely-shaped occipital condyles. It's seems like it was a very good design plan right from the start.

Sauropods

Next, let's take a look at the sauropod dinosaurs. Sauropods are the largest land animals in history, with some of them (such as *Argentinosaurus* and *Patagotitan mayorum*) exceeding 115 feet and weighing over 140,000 pounds.[9]

Figure 4. Sauropod Dinosaur[10]

Figure 5 shows a leg from a massive sauropod dinosaur. Do you notice how the bone at the top (the humerus) is made of one solid piece, followed by the two bones below the knee (the ulna and radius), followed by five foot bones, then five toes? This "large and solid" to "smaller and spread out" system allowed these massive creatures to distribute their weight and walk on mobile pillars. Given that estimates of some sauropods exceed 120 feet and 140,000 pounds, it would certainly take an amazing design plan for this creature to walk! Unlike other dinosaurs, sauropods could lock their legs straight, conserving energy.

Figure 5. Royal Terrell Museum (Author)

Where are all of the sauropods that don't have this weight-bearing design? They don't exist. All ~300 that have been found so far are made this way.[11] As we'll soon see, this is just the tip of the iceberg when it comes to the design features that need to be present *at the same time* for these creatures to live.

Job 40 and the Behemoth

It's no wonder that the Book of Job (the oldest book of the Bible, written about 3,500 years ago[12]) refers to Behemoth—a sauropod dinosaur—as the "chief" or "first in rank" of all God's creation. Consider the description of this animal from Job 40:6–24:

> Then the Lord answered Job out of the whirlwind, and said: "Now prepare yourself like a man; I will question you, and you shall answer Me... Look at Behemoth, which I **made along with you** and which feeds on grass like an ox. What **strength it has in its loins**, what **power in the muscles of its belly**! Its **tail sways like a cedar**; the **sinews of its thighs are close-knit**. Its **bones are tubes of bronze**, its **limbs like rods of iron**. It **ranks first among the works of God**, yet its Maker can approach it with his sword. The hills bring it their produce, and all the wild animals play nearby. Under the lotus plants it lies, hidden among the reeds in the marsh. The lotuses conceal it in their shadow; the poplars by the stream surround it. **A raging river does not alarm it; it is secure, though the Jordan should surge against its mouth**. Can anyone capture it by the eyes, or trap it and pierce its nose?

In context, Job and his philosopher friends just finished over 30 chapters of dialogue trying to explain God and why He would allow such hardships into Job's life. Then God shows up in a whirlwind, tells Job to "brace himself like a man" and says that He would be the one asking Job the questions for a while (KJV: "Gird up thy loins now like a man: I will demand of thee, and declare thou unto me"). Then, for four chapters straight, God asks Job 77 rhetorical questions that are all about Creation. After explaining to Job that He is the master designer of space and earth, God describes 13 of His created animals, such as an ostrich, horse, and deer, then caps off the discussion by telling Job about His two grandest creations: Behemoth and Leviathan. God calls Behemoth the "first of all of His ways," using the Hebrew term (re'shiyth), which means *first in a rank*, the *chief*, the *most supreme* of His creative works.

When God says to Job, sit down, brace yourself, and now I will tell you of the chief of all my works—the biggest, most amazing land creature I ever made—he's not talking about a common animal like a hippo or a crocodile. When we scan through all land-dwelling creatures—both living and extinct—which one comes up as the "first in rank," the most colossal or the chief? Clearly the sauropod dinosaur. Pairing God's Word that Behemoth is the grandest creature He ever made with the fact that sauropods are the largest land creatures we've ever found should give us a clue to Behemoth's identity.

Sauropods were huge. The largest one found to date (named *Patagotitan mayorum*) was over 120 feet long—that's 10 freeway lanes across! At a weight of 76 tons, it's a wonder these creatures could even walk! Let's start by looking at one of their unique design features: their long necks.

The necks of the sauropod dinosaurs were by far the longest of any animal, six times longer than that of the world record giraffe and five times longer than those of all other terrestrial animals.[13]

Mamenchisaurus youngi
(Pi et al, 1996)

Figure 6. *Mamenchisaurus* a Type of Sauropod Dinosaur.[14]

The engineering required for a living creature to have such a long neck has perplexed dinosaur researchers for years—the physics just don't seem to work because the necks would be too heavy for their length. Leading sauropod researcher, Dr. Matthew Wedel notes: "They were marvels of biological engineering, and that efficiency of design is especially evident in their vertebrae, the bones that make up the backbone."[15] After spending years studying the long necks of sauropods, Dr. Wedel made a discovery that was so significant it earned him the Fourth International Award in Paleontology Research. In short, Dr. Wedel revealed that the vertebrae of these massive sauropods were pneumatic—they were *filled with air*![16]

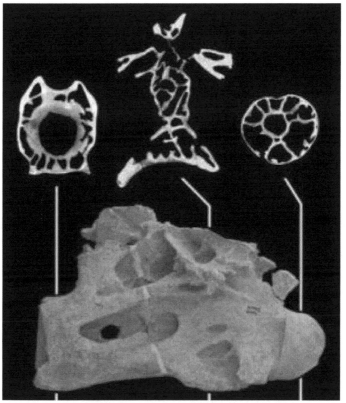

Figure 7. Apatosaurus Vertebra Showing Most of Its Space
Filled with Air Cavities.[17]

Dr. Wedel started researching these air-filled vertebrae
as an undergraduate researcher in Oklahoma, where he spent his
Saturdays running dinosaur bones through the CT scanner at his
local hospital. There, he discovered that "one of Sauropod's
four and a half foot vertebrae would have been surprisingly
light and could reach 90% air by volume!"[18]

Figure 8. A 4-1/2-Foot Sauropod Vertebra That Could Reach 90% Air by Volume.

More exhaustive studies by Dr. Wedel and others have revealed that the vertebrae of most sauropods were often 50–60% air by volume, with some as high as 90% (see Figure 8).[19] While Dr. Wedel estimates that this would only reduce the overall weight of some of these creatures by 8–10%, most of the weight would be removed from the critical areas of the neck, where extra weight would have been challenging for the creature to lift its head, eat, or turn around.

Yet there's more—these big creatures needed *light* vertebrae to enable them to lift their heads—but these extra-long necks also needed to be *designed* in such a way that the animal could eat, drink, and move its head without its neck folding in half or pinching vital nerves or even the trachea (for breathing) or esophagus (for eating). Having an extra-light structure was only part of the solution.

Take a close-up look at the neck vertebrae of these creatures (shown in Figure 9). Do you notice the shape of the vertebrae, and how they have protruding bones that face the same direction?

Figure 9. Royal Terrell Museum (Author)

Each of these protruding structures served as anchoring points for the connective soft tissue that held the neck together. Dinosaur researchers have also tried to figure out how the tendons, ligaments, and muscles must have been assembled for this creature to have a stable neck system. They've even proposed several complex models that try to demonstrate how everything might have fit together (Figure 10).

21

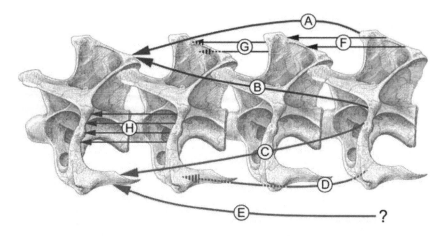

Figure 10. Sauropod Vertebrae (Taylor & Wedel, 2012).[20]

Taylor and Wedel developed a model showing what the connections that hold together the vertebrae might have looked like (Figure 10). The muscle passing behind the bone is shown using dashed lines; muscles inserting on the epiphyses (attachment areas for several neck muscles) are shown with lines C, D, E; muscles inserting on the cervical ribs are shown with lines F and G; and muscles inserting on the neural spine are shown with line H.

Does this look complicated? Yes, indeed—but that's only the *muscular* system. The *ligaments* and *tendons* still need to fit into the design in an amazing way for this creature to *swallow* and *breathe* through this complex neck system.

For this creature to eat, breathe, and move its long neck, the 12+ neck vertebrae[21] of sauropods had to be *interlocking* and *twistable*. Further, the vertebrae had to have anchoring points in *just the right places* for muscles and ligaments to connect in such a way to prevent the neck from pinching veins, nerves, trachea, and the esophagus.

While their air-charged vertebrae may solve the puzzle of how they could lift and move their massive heads and necks, it doesn't solve the challenge of how they could possibly inhale enough oxygen through their tiny nostrils, which were only about twice the size of those on a living horse! How can a 140,000+ pound animal inhale enough oxygen through such tiny nostrils? Perhaps they thrived better in a world before Noah's Flood when the oxygen levels were likely higher. We'll cover more on this topic later.

God even describes Behemoth's diet: eating grass like an ox. In 2005 researchers found grass in sauropod coprolites in India, and some palaeobotanists are even saying that this will cause a "rewrite in our understanding of dinosaur evolution," because evolution holds that grass didn't evolve until millions of years after the dinosaurs had gone extinct.[22]

God describes Behemoth's strength in his hips, and power in his stomach muscles. Again, we have a strong clue that Behemoth was a sauropod dinosaur because, while many animals have strong hips and stomach muscles, none were as strong as the sauropod! The muscular structure around the hips and stomach that were necessary for sauropods to move, walk, turn, and eat would be incredible! In fact, for some sauropods, like the Diplodocus, its highest point of its core body was the hips and its whole body balanced on the hips, front-to-back. Diplodocus was able to rear up on its back legs and balance on its tail like a tripod, making use of the hips to support not just the back half of its body, but the front half, too. This required enormous strength in the hip and stomach muscles, considering they lifted tons of its own body into the air. Below the hips was an incredible weight distribution system that went from a massive femur (which in some cases was nearly 8 feet long), to two shin bones, then five foot bones, and then five toes.

Behemoth's tail also closely matched those of sauropods. God describes that he "moves his tail like a cedar tree" and follows this by stating, "the sinews of his thighs are tightly knit." Paleontologists have learned from the muscle attachment locations in their bones that the tightly-knit structure of Behemoth's thighs and hips actually made his tail sway from side-to-side with each step, much as a cedar tree does when it sways in the wind![23] Tail drag marks are only rarely found behind sauropod footprints, indicating their tails were raised

23

while they walked. It's difficult to think of a creature that fits this Biblical description better than a sauropod dinosaur.

God describes his bones "like beams of bronze." Most Bible versions translate this phrase as "tubes of bronze," "conduits of bronze," or "pipes of brass," which conveys both "strength" and being hollow like a channel or a tube. This matches the fact that that sauropods had the largest leg bones of any animal, and they are in fact just like tubes of metal, having a hard outer casing and spongy marrow and veins on the inside.

Then God says that its "ribs are like bars of iron." Unlike much of the sauropod's skeleton that was spongy and filled with air for weight savings, its ribs were *fully ossified*— they were made of solid bone![24] Again, there is a perfect match between God's description of Behemoth and a sauropod dinosaur.

God even describes Behemoth's habitat: "He lies under the lotus trees, in a covert of reeds and marsh. The lotus trees cover him with their shade" and "The willows by the brook surround him." This was a creature that had to be near lots of green food—living in a lush, tropical environment. Large sauropods had to eat a half a ton of vegetation every day, and they likely had to eat all day long to consume this amount of food.

Next God says: "Indeed the river may rage, yet he is not disturbed; He is confident, though the Jordan gushes into his mouth." Why would God point out that this animal can stand in a rushing river? Lots of animals can do this, depending on the size of the rushing river. In this case, God said, "the river may *rage*, yet he is *not disturbed"* and that Behemoth is confident even though this raging river should gush into his mouth. The Jordan river is the largest river in Palestine and it currently flows at only 15% of the rate it flowed in the past.[25] Even so, in the winter this river would be incredibly difficult to cross, and it would take a *very* sizable animal to stand *undisturbed* in the rushing current and, even more, let the current gush into its mouth! Some of the larger sauropods stood over 20 feet at the shoulders and weighed over 70 tons. Creatures of this size and mass could withstand a raging river better than any others.

Even with all this evidence, some say that Behemoth was a just a mythical creature. Why would God try to display His awesome creative power by describing something that never existed? Anyone can do that. And why would God say that Behemoth was the "chief" of all His creations after describing 13 real, still-living animals in the same passage? Why go through all the trouble to describe Behemoth as a grass-eating animal that lies peacefully in the shadow of the river plants along with his physical description, diet, and habitat—all of which happen to fit a known creature: a sauropod dinosaur?

Certain Bible footnotes[26] state that Behemoth was a hippo, elephant, or crocodile but these do not come close to matching all 14 characteristics God used to describe Behemoth. They certainly are not the "first in rank" or "chief" of God's creations. Would God tell Job to "gird up his loins" to behold the "chief of his creations" just to show off a hippo? An elephant? These creatures were plentiful! They also don't have tails that sway like cedar trees, and both of these animals have been captured and killed by man throughout history.

Table 1 lists 14 characteristics of this creature that are provided in Job 40, and a sauropod dinosaur seems to fit the description better than any other creature, alive or extinct.

Table 1. Behemoth Description from Job 40

Behemoth Description (Job 40)	Sauropod	Hippo	Crocodile
1 - "made along with" man	YES	YES	YES
2 - eats grass like an ox	YES	YES	NO
3 - strength in hips/stomach muscles	YES	NO	NO
4 - he moves his tail like a cedar	YES	NO	NO
5 - sinews of his thighs are tightly knit	YES	YES	YES
6 - bones are like beams of bronze	YES	NO	NO
7 - ribs like bars of iron	YES	MAYBE	MAYBE
8 - "chief/first" in rank of all God's creations	YES	NO	NO
9 - mountains yield food for him, and all the beasts of the field play there	YES	MAYBE	NO
10 - lies under lotus trees, in reeds/marsh	YES	NO	NO
11 - lotus trees cover him with their shade; willows by the brook surround him	YES	YES	YES
12 - The river may rage, yet he is not disturbed	YES	NO	NO
13 - He is confident, though the Jordan gushes into his mouth	YES	MAYBE	MAYBE
14 - unapproachable by anyone but its maker	YES	NO	NO

God says that only Behemoth's Creator can approach him, that he cannot be captured by humans when he is on watch, and that no one can use barbs to pierce his nose. These impossibilities fit sauropod dinosaurs better than other animals because of their towering heads and huge size. With a head that reached over 40 feet high, it could see people coming from far away. Its massive tail also makes him unapproachable. Based on what we know from fossils, some sauropods could cover a 200-foot circle with deadly force using their tails which could be over 50-feet long and weigh over 13,000 pounds.[27] Studies have shown that some sauropods could probably create sonic booms with their tails—just like a whip.[28]

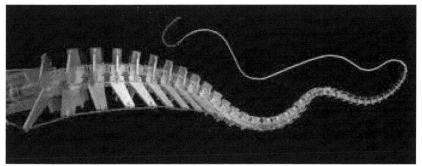

Figure 11. Study Demonstrated that Sauropod Tails Could Create Sonic Booms (D. Sivam / P. Currie / N. Myhrvold)

Figure 12. Behemoth's Tail Was One Reason Behemoth Was Unapproachable by Anyone but God, His Creator [29]

It's not by chance that God says to Job that Behemoth can *only be approached by his creator*. Good luck even getting near this creature to put a snare in its nose. To this day, elephants and hippos are surrounded by hunters and killed, but sauropods better fit this passage because they are simply unapproachable.

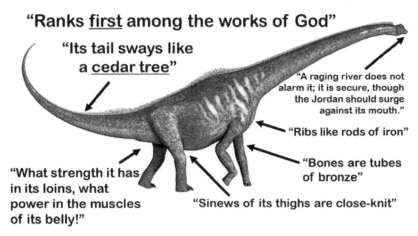

"Ranks <u>first</u> among the works of God"

"Its tail sways like a <u>cedar tree</u>"

"A raging river does not alarm it; it is secure, though the Jordan should surge against its mouth."

"Ribs like rods of iron"

"Bones are tubes of bronze"

"What strength it has in its loins, what power in the muscles of its belly!"

"Sinews of its thighs are close-knit"

Figure 13. Behemoth in Job Chapter 40.

This section has reviewed the incredible design features that all need to be present for these creatures to live. And the fact that these features—weight-bearing hips, legs, feet, and toes, incredible air-filled vertebrae, and others—show up already formed in the ~300 sauropods that have been found! Yes, there is variability within the sauropod kind, but these animals have been grouped by these (and other) common design characteristics. If God Himself created these animals and placed them on the Earth, then no wonder they had every aspect of their essential design features already in place and fully integrated from the start. The next dinosaur evidence that fits the Bible reviews the fossils.

Evidence #2: Lack of Dinosaur Ancestors and Transitions

The fact that secular dinosaur researchers cannot find the *ancestors* (from which the dinosaurs supposedly evolved) and the *transitions* between the different dinosaurs confirms the Biblical account that they were spontaneously placed here by God (each after their own *kind*—see Genesis 1:25). Figure 14 shows a reconstructed graphic from a leading dinosaur reference book: *The Encyclopedia of Dinosaurs.*[30]

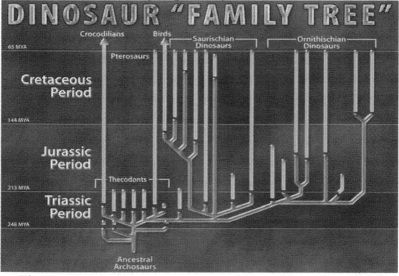

Figure 14. Dinosaur Ancestors and Transitions from *The Encyclopedia of Dinosaurs.*

In small print at the bottom of the chart in the *Encyclopedia of Dinosaurs* it states: "**Tinted areas indicate solid fossil evidence**" (these "tinted areas" are shown in Figure 14 by the broken lines above the tree that starts from the bottom, starting with "Ancestral Archosaurs"). Notice that fossil evidence only exists for the various kinds of dinosaurs themselves, with **no** precursors and **no** transitions! Indeed, the tree that starts at the bottom of the chart is a **theoretical** one because the "real data" based on actual dinosaur fossils only shows the different kinds of dinosaurs, that are always found after their own kind—just like the Bible says in Genesis 1:25: "God made the beasts of the Earth *after their kind...*"

Medical Doctor Carl Werner has done extensive research that confirms there are no ancestors or transitions for the dinosaurs. Dr. Werner spent 17 years traveling to the best museums and dig sites around the globe photographing thousands of original fossils and the actual fossil layers where they were found, and interviewing museum staff about this very question.

One of the examples of this is found in Dr. Werner's book, *Evolution: The Grand Experiment* where he provides a photo taken at the famous Chicago Field Museum. This museum display shows the theoretical evolution of dinosaurs, starting with the "common ancestor" and moving through the "transitions" covering a supposed time span of about 155 million years. There's just one major problem with this museum display—when inserting the number of dinosaur ancestors (at the beginning of the display) and the number of transitions at each of the branches, the display actually proves the *opposite* of what's intended. See Figure 15 that shows the display with these counts added.

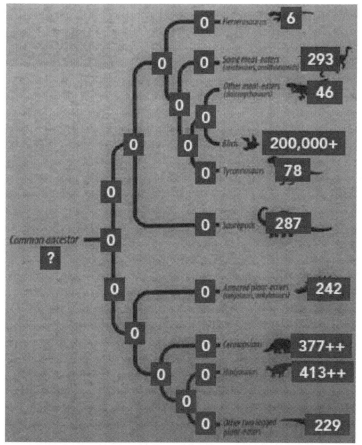

Figure 15. Dinosaur Evolution Display from the Chicago Field Museum (Counts Added).

After spending 17 years cataloging fossils at museums and interviewing hundreds of secular scientists about the fossil evidence of evolution, Dr. Werner found that they could not agree on a single common ancestor for all dinosaurs or any of the key supposed transitions between dinosaur kinds. Instead, each basic kind suddenly appeared on Earth. Notice that all of the supposed transitions between the various dinosaur kinds have a 0 next to them. Dr. Werner could not find a *single* in-between transition that evolutionists can agree on. It's almost like someone just miraculously put dinosaurs here on Earth, each to reproduce after its own kind, just like the Bible says.

Dr. Werner explains the significance of Figure 15 by stating, "Over 30 million dinosaur bones have been discovered. Of these, thousands of individual dinosaur skeletons have been collected by museums representing over 700 dinosaur species. Yet, not a single direct ancestor has been found for any dinosaur. Also, the proposed theoretical common ancestor for all dinosaurs has not been found."[31]

For example, Dr. Viohl, Curator of the Famous Jura Museum in Germany states the following about pterosaurs: "We know only little about the evolution of pterosaurs. The ancestors are not known... When the pterosaurs first appear in the geologic record, they were *completely perfect*. They were *perfect pterosaurs*"[32] (emphasis added). The same is true for every dinosaur group reflected on the chart.

If the theory of evolution is true, and one type of dinosaur evolved into another over millions of years, dinosaur evolution charts in textbooks around the world should be filled with numerous examples of dinosaur kinds evolving into others over the supposed 155 million years they were on Earth. But actual data shows the *exact* opposite.

Now that museums around the world have collected over 100,000 dinosaurs,[33] the number of "transitional" dinosaurs going between the various categories should be evenly distributed if evolution were true. But this is not the case. Even when interviewing numerous leading, evolution-believing scientists at these museums, Dr. Werner could not find a single scientist to offer any transitions. Instead, Dr. Werner found secular scientists stating the opposite. For example, Dr. David Weishampel, Editor of the encyclopedic reference book *The Dinosauria* wrote, "From my reading of the fossil record of dinosaurs, **no direct ancestors have been discovered for any dinosaur species**. Alas, my list of dinosaurian ancestors is an **empty** one." It appears that dinosaur evolution finds no basis in fossils.

Evidence #3: Dinosaur Anatomy Shows They Were Better-Suited for the Pre-Flood World

Biblical creationists and evolutionists both agree that the world in which dinosaurs lived was *different* than the world we live in today.[34] While we may not agree on *how* it was different and *when* it was created and changed, we at least agree that Earth has not always been like it is today.

Volumes of evolutionary science papers and books have been written on the atmospheric conditions in which these massive and unusual dinosaurs existed. Some books, such as Peter Ward's *Out of Thin Air: Dinosaurs, Birds, and Earth's Ancient Atmosphere,*[35] have attempted to describe what this ancient world must have been like.

Ward, speaking from the evolutionary viewpoint, believes that changes in oxygen and carbon dioxide levels in the atmosphere over millions of years led to significant changes that allowed the expansion of different types of plants and animals. The basic idea is that the types of plants and animals that were suited for each period of Earth's changing condition survived, and those that were not died off.

Biblical Creation holds that God created a perfect initial world with no death, no carnivory, and no "survival of the fittest."[36] Further, animals were created to reproduce—just as we observe today—after their "own kind." Creationists also believe that this perfect world held out until it was marred by the sin of Adam and Eve, which brought death, suffering, bloodshed, and disease.[37] Geographically, this pre-Flood world had only a single landmass (Rodinia) until the Flood broke the continents apart less than 1,700 years after Creation.[38]

Biblical creationists have presented many pre-Flood climate models over the years, with many of them falling under the heading of "Canopy Models." While several variants exist, all canopy models interpret the "waters above" (firmament) in Genesis 1:7 to be some type of water-based canopy encircling the Earth that existed from the beginning of creation until the

Flood. As scientific models, these ideas held promise to explain the pre-Flood climate, but they also produce many conditions (e.g., extreme surface temperatures) that make them problematic. While these models and others exist, we ultimately don't know what the pre-Flood world was like because we weren't there. Further, the Bible only gives a few insights to what the pre-Flood world was like:

- Before the Fall, the atmosphere was *perfect* for sustaining life in all ways (Genesis 1:31) and there was no death (Genesis 2:17; Romans 5:12; 1 Corinthians 15:22).
- Earth's atmosphere likely had sunlight and temperature variations within the days and nights (Genesis 3:8).
- Given that Adam and Eve were told to be "fruitful and multiply and fill the earth" (Genesis 1:27; 3:21) and they were "naked and unashamed" before the Fall (Genesis 2:25), it appears they had no need of clothing before the Fall.
- The Flood ruptured Rodinia and rearranged continents, creating extreme weather on the high mountains that were pushed up that the Flood elevated (Psalm 104:8).
- Genesis 2:5–6 states, "For the Lord God had not caused it to rain on the earth, and there was no man to till the ground; but a mist went up from the earth and watered the whole face of the ground." While some interpret this passage to mean that there was no rain until the Flood (a possibility), this passage is at least clear that before the Sixth Day of Creation Week, God had watered the plants with a mist and had not yet caused rain or created a man to till the ground.
- Because the rainbow was given to mark a new covenant between God and the Earth (to never again Flood the entire earth) (Genesis 9:13), there is the possibility that Earth's climate was changed after (and by) the Flood to

allow rainbows.[39] However, God may have used an existing phenomena as a sign of His covenant.

These insights point to the idea that the pre-Flood world was quite different than the post-Flood world of today. The New Testament also acknowledges this distinction (2 Peter 3:6: "by which the world that then existed perished, being flooded with water"). Next let's turn to some clues in the fossil record that may also indicate that the pre-Flood world wasn't like today's world.

- Giant land beasts, such as sauropod dinosaurs that grew as large as 115 feet and 200,000 pounds.
- Giant flying reptiles, pterosaurs, with over 50-foot wingspans (e.g., *Quetzalcoatlus*).
- Giant dragonflies with 2-1/2 foot wingspans and 17-inch bodies (*Meganeura*).
- Mushrooms that grew over 20-feet high (*Prototaxites*).[40]
- Giant millipedes that grew over eight feet long (*Arthropleura*).

The above list could be much longer; these are just a few examples. Biblical creationists and evolutionists agree that these giant creatures and plants existed. Indeed, they are in the fossil record for everyone to evaluate, regardless of the worldview lens through which they are viewed. We also agree that these giant creatures and plants existed in a *different version of the Earth*, with evolutionists placing this version millions of years ago and Biblical creationists placing it before the Flood, about 4,400 years ago. Let's briefly review each of these examples.

Giant Land Beasts (Sauropods)

In the previous section, we looked at the massive, unmatched size of the sauropod dinosaurs, but we left out one important feature of this magnificent animal until now—*how they breathed*. Many who have studied this issue would agree that these creatures would have a difficult time staying alive very long in today's current atmosphere with only 21% oxygen levels. This is, at least in part, due to this animal's extremely small nasal passages compared to its enormous body size. See Figure 16.

"An 80-foot-long brontosaurus had a set of nostrils about the same size as a horse's... There were some serious problems with trying to get air into that animal."
– Richard Hengst, Purdue University Physiologist

Figure 16. Giant Sauropod[41]

Do you notice the immense size of the sauropod's body compared to its nasal passages? While the nasal structures of the different sauropods vary, one consistent trait is the extremely small nasal passages compared to their body size. The explanation given by some evolutionists is simply that the ancient Earth had higher oxygen levels (35%),[42] and when the oxygen level dropped, the dinosaurs died out (one of many dinosaur extinction theories offered by evolutionists).[43]

Scientists that have studied sauropod anatomy have recognized this challenge, stating: "An 80-foot-long brontosaurus had a set of nostrils about the same size as a horse's ... there were some serious problems with trying to get air into that animal. Dinosaurs could not have existed without having more oxygen in the air to start with."[44]

So just what were the oxygen levels of the pre-Flood world? To be fair, we really don't know. Some Biblical creationists have theorized, at least when it comes to giant insects that are in the fossil record that grew to enormous sizes, that oxygen levels might have played a part. For example, when discussing the fact that pre-Flood insects grew much larger than today and the possibility that higher oxygen levels may be one possible explanation, Drs. Carl Wieland and Jonathan Sarfati stated, "This may be because the pre-Flood world carried more oxygen-producing vegetation."[45]

Giant Flying Reptiles (Pterosaurs)

One of the largest flying reptiles is *Quetzalcoatlus*, which was named after the Mesoamerican feathered serpent god, Quetzalcoatl. Many studies have attempted to estimate this creature's wingspan, with most estimates coming in over 36 feet.[46]

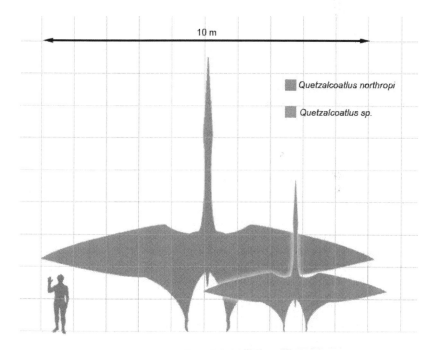

Figure 17. Quetzalcoatlus Wingspan[47]

The wingspan, however, is not what puzzles scientists about this giant—it's the *large wingspan given its weight.* While estimates vary, some studies estimate the weight of the larger specimens discovered to exceed 500 pounds.[48] That's likely too much weight for a flying creature to bear and still be able to fly. Several studies have investigated how these massive creatures could fly, with some reports even titled, "This Pterodactyl was so big it couldn't fly" and opening sentences such as "Bad news dragon riders: Your dragon can't take off."[49]

Scientists who have studied and published on this extensively have even admitted: "…it is now generally agreed that even the largest pterosaurs could not have flown in today's skies" and have offered explanations such as "warmer climate" or "higher levels of atmospheric oxygen" as reasons it could have flown only during the era in which it lived.[50]

Some secular studies that have investigated air bubbles trapped in amber that was dated to the "ancient world in which dinosaurs lived," have found *both* increased pressure as well as greater oxygen levels: "'One implication is that the atmospheric pressure of the Earth would have been much greater during the Cretaceous era, when the bubbles formed in the resin. A dense atmosphere could also explain how the ungainly pterosaur, with its stubby body and wing span of up to 11 meters, could have stayed airborne,' he said. 'The spread of angiosperms, flowering plants, during the Cretaceous era could have caused the high oxygen levels[51] reported by Berner and Landis.'"[52]

Interesting—giant sauropods couldn't likely breathe in today's world, giant flying reptiles that could not have flown in today's atmosphere—what's next? Giant dragonflies.

Giant Dragonflies (Meganeura)

The largest dragonfly species alive today (*Megaloprepus caerulatus*) has a wingspan of up to seven inches and a body up to five inches long. Based on the fossil record, the largest pre-Flood dragonflies (*Meganeura*) had wingspans up to 2-1/2 feet and a 17-inch body. See Figure 18.

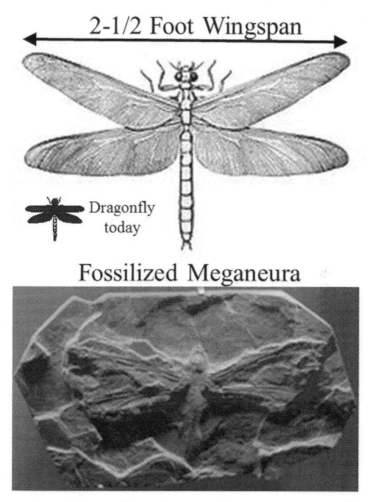

2-1/2 Foot Wingspan

Dragonfly today

Fossilized Meganeura

Figure 18. Giant Pre-Flood Dragonfly (*Meganeura*).[53]

In October 2006, *Science Daily* publicized a study led by Arizona State University staff titled "Giant Insects Might Reign if Only There Was More Oxygen in the Air."[54] The article claims:

> The delicate lady bug in your garden could be frighteningly large if only there was a greater

concentration of oxygen in the air, a new study concludes. The study adds support to the theory that some insects were much larger during the late Paleozoic period because they had a much richer oxygen supply, said the study's lead author Alexander Kaiser. The Paleozoic period…was a time of huge and abundant plant life and rather large insects—dragonflies had two-and-a-half-foot wing spans, for example. The air's oxygen content was 35% during this period, compared to the 21% we breathe now, Kaiser said.

This research lends evidence to the fact that the pre-Flood world was different than the one we live in today.

One study conducted in 2010 by researchers at Arizona State University tested this "more oxygen = bigger insects" theory directly by raising 12 different types of insects in simulated atmospheres with various oxygen levels. Their study included three sets of 75 dragonflies in atmospheres containing 12%, 21%, and 31% oxygen levels and their experiment confirmed that dragonflies grow bigger with more oxygen.[55] While there are likely a host of reasons why the pre-Flood dragonflies grew much larger than those today, especially genetic bottlenecking at the Genesis Flood, it is quite interesting to see the clear dichotomy between larger creatures of many types before the Flood compared to the animals alive today.

Giant Mushrooms (Prototaxites) and Plants

You don't need to read many secular-based books about the "ancient Earth" before learning about gigantic vegetation that existed supposedly millions of years ago. One example is the *Prototaxites* (see Figure 19). Some reports even state that these gigantic (now extinct) mushroom-like plants covered much of the Earth and "dotted the ancient landscape."[56]

Figure 19. *Prototaxites*

First discovered by a Canadian in 1859, no one seemed to know what they were. But after 130 years of debate whether this plant was a lichen, fungus, or some kind of tree, scientists have come to some level of agreement that it was essentially a "gigantic early mushroom."

Plants and fungi like these puzzle evolutionists, such as Kevin Boyce of Geophysical Sciences at University of Chicago, who stated, "A 20-foot tall fungus doesn't make any sense. Neither does a 20-foot tall algae make any sense, but here's the fossil."[57]

From a Biblical creationist standpoint, this is simply a gigantic pre-Flood fungus that was created to thrive in the pre-Flood world, but not now. In a temperate, pre-Flood world where wearing clothing was (originally) "optional," it's no wonder that giant fungus and plants like this could have thrived.

Giant Millipedes (Arthropleura)

Giant millipedes (called *Arthropleura*) that grew to be over eight feet long[58] used to crawl around before the Flood in what became northeastern America and Scotland. While evolutionists assign "millions of years" to these creatures, all we can know for total certainty is that they died. The larger species of this group are the largest known land invertebrates of all time. Evolutionists attribute their grand size to different pressures and/or oxygen levels of Earth's ancient past.[59]

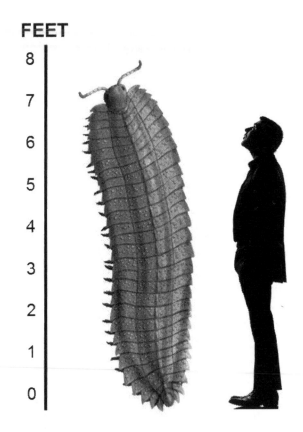

Figure 20. Giant Pre-Flood Millipedes (*Arthropleura*)

Evidence #4: The Vast Extent of the Fossil Record

President of Answers in Genesis, Ken Ham, has become well-known for making this statement: "If there really was a Global Flood, what would the evidence be? Billions of dead things, buried in rock layers, laid down by water all over the Earth." This is exactly what we see.

For example, the Paleobiology Database (PaleoBioDB) is a free, searchable database that is designed to "provide global, collection-based occurrence and taxonomic data for organisms of all geological ages."[60] This database includes 183,739 fossil *collections* totaling 1,323,009 *occurrences* (with each "occurrence" ranging from a few fossils to numerous). From a Biblical Creation standpoint, the Genesis Flood deposited the vast majority of these fossils. The circles in Figure 21 shows the extent of the known fossil record.

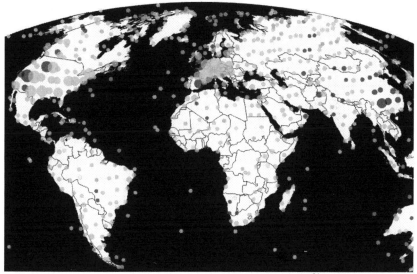

Figure 21. Paleobiology Database[61]

If the untestable assumptions that hold up the ideas of radiometric dating are not true (and we believe they are not[62]), then Figure 21 displays a massive, watery graveyard, most of which was filled during the year-long Genesis Flood.

The number of dinosaur "mass graves" around the world is astounding. These fossil graveyards contain a mixture of many different kinds of fossils that have been *transported by large volumes of water* (see Figure 22). Modern, small-scale debris flows offer examples of what likely entrained in some cases millions of animals. Like a giant water wing, a debris flow

43

carries its load largely undisturbed inside, as it rides upon a watery cushion either underwater or over land. As soon as the flow slows to a certain speed, turbulence overwhelms the load and it drops in place.

Figure 22. Fossil Graveyard Example

Bone fossils typically occur as broken fragments. They were violently carried along with enormous mounds of mud and shifting sediments. By studying some of these fossil graveyards, we can gather clues that will demonstrate that the Flood was in fact catastrophic and worldwide, as stated in Genesis 7:20–23:

> The waters rose and covered the mountains to a depth of more than fifteen cubits [at least 22 feet]. *Every living thing* that moved on land perished—birds, livestock, wild animals, *all the creatures* that swarm over the earth, and *all mankind. Everything* on dry land that had the breath of life in its nostrils died. *Every living thing* on the face of the earth was wiped out; people and animals and the creatures that move

along the ground and the birds were wiped from the earth. *Only Noah was left,* and those with him in the ark. (emphasis added)

If this passage in Genesis is true, we would expect to find *billions of dead things buried in rock layers laid down by water all over the earth.*[63] And this is exactly what we find *all over the world.*

Another profound example is Dinosaur National Monument in Utah, which is only a part of the 700,000-square mile Morrison Formation, a geologic unit that has spawned excavations of more than a hundred dinosaur quarries.[64]

Figure 23. Aerial extent of the Morrison Formation.[65]

What type of catastrophe could possibly bury hundreds of massive bone beds in this 700,000-square mile area, all at once? It could represent an enormous, ancient debris flow that only a worldwide watery catastrophe could reasonably explain.

Evidence #5: Dinosaurs Were Buried Furiously (Disarticulated)

Only about 3,000 of the dinosaur fossils that have been collected represent "articulated"[66] (bones still in place) animals. Because over 100,000 dinosaurs have been found, this represents only about 3% of the dinosaur fossil record.[67] So these animals did not die peacefully. Whatever wiped them out was *sudden* and *violent*.

I will never forget walking around at Dinosaur Provincial Park in Canada, which is one of the largest mass dinosaur graves in the world. In just this one area, over 32,000 fossil specimens have been found, representing 35 species, 34 genera, and 12 families of dinosaurs. Astonishingly, dinosaur fossils intermingle with fish, turtles, marsupial and other mammals, and amphibians. Also, only 300 complete animals have been found! The large majority were scrambled, pulverized, and blended together, as if the world became an enormous washing machine.

While walking around the outdoor exhibits, one display caught my daughter's eye. It was a large hadrosaur, a "duck-bill" dinosaur, that they left in the ground, exactly as it was found, covered with mud and twisted around like it went through a blender before it was buried. A young boy pushed a button to play the audio explanation provided by the museum that described the evolutionary idea about how the animal died. Their explanation was that a large tropical storm caused the rivers to rise and the dinosaurs to drown—one after the other—as each blindly followed the other to their death (thousands of them).[68]

This is when my daughter had her epiphany: "You've got to be kidding me!" she exclaimed. "Look at all these dead dinosaurs—they're everywhere! And they're buried in countless tons of sediment—how's a local rainstorm going to do that? Noah's Flood is a much better explanation!" She's onto something. If rainstorms explain this, then why don't they deposit and fossilize even smaller creatures today? This dinosaur graveyard was massive—spanning a 2.3 square kilometer area. Imagine walking around an area this size with thousands of buried Centrosaurs (estimates exceed 10,000 Centrosaurs alone!).[69] It was an eerie feeling!

Evidence #6: Dinosaurs Were Quickly Buried in Mud

The very fact that we have so many preserved dinosaur fossils shows that they were buried quickly because fossilization requires rapid burial in muddy ground. The fossil record is full of dinosaurs that suddenly died in watery graves around the world, with many of them found in the famous "death pose" with their necks arched back, as if drowning in mud.[70]

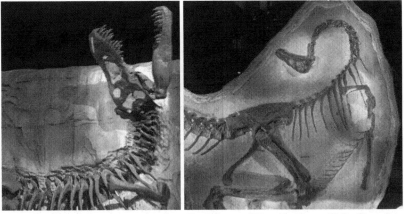

Figure 24. Dinosaurs in the Common "Death Pose," Indicating Rapid Burial and Suffocation (Royal Terrell Museum, Author).

Evidence #7: Dinosaurs Were Buried Simultaneously, Fleeing in Groups

Sauropod and Triceratops Graveyards

From a Biblical viewpoint, the Paleobiology Database is useful for finding where extinct animal groups (like dinosaurs) may have lived before they were wiped out by the Flood. For example, Figure 25 plots both the sauropod and triceratops dinosaur fossils that have been found in the Midwestern United States. Isn't it interesting that these totally different dinosaur types were simultaneously wiped out and buried in the *same areas*? Something stopped these two very large dinosaur types dead in their tracks and buried them in mud, preserving their fossils for us to find today.

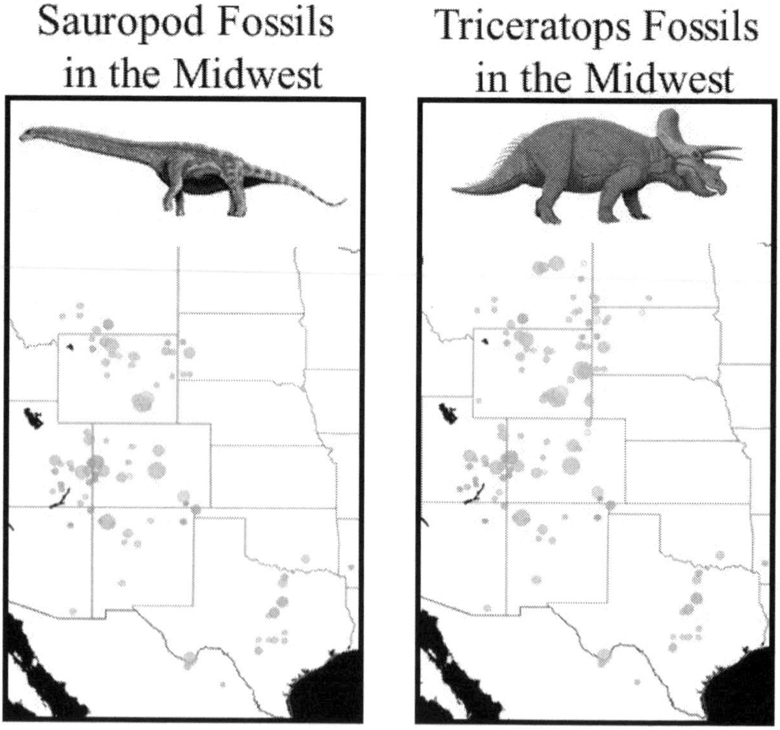

Figure 25. Sauropod and Triceratops Graveyards.

Sauropods and Triceratops are some of the largest dinosaurs to ever live. What type of event would it take to bury these massive creatures in mud so quickly that they would be disarticulated and preserved for us to find today—locked in mud that hardened into rock before getting scavenged? Slow, gradually-rising creeks or rivers? A sudden worldwide Flood explains more.

Thousands of Buried Centrosaurs in Hilda, Canada

The famous Hilda bone beds in Canada, briefly discussed above, actually include 14 dinosaur "bone beds" that contain thousands of buried Centrosaurs *found in the same stratigraphic column* (a term used in geology to describe the vertical location of rocks in a particular area). The authors who completed the most extensive study of the area described the sediment in which these dinosaurs are buried as "mudstone rich in organic matter deposited on the tract of land separating two ancient rivers."[71] They also concluded that each of the 14 bone beds was actually part of a single, massive "mega-bone bed" that occupied 2.3 square kilometers—almost a square mile! Stop and think about this for a minute. How did thousands of dinosaurs—of the same species—get herded up and simultaneously buried in mud?

These authors even concluded that the massive bone beds were formed when a herd of Centrosaurs *drowned during a flood*. These bone beds are also found with aquatic vertebrates such as fish, turtles, and crocodiles, showing that water was definitely involved in their transport and burial. In addition, almost no teeth marks indicated any scavenging after these animals died, probably because most of them died at the same time.[72]

Massive Dinosaur Graveyard Found in China

An online article on Discovery.com describes the dinosaur graveyard in China as the largest in the world, writing, "Researchers say they can't understand why so many animals gathered in what is today the city of Zhucheng to die." Thousands of dinosaur bones stack on top of each other in "incredible density," then they "suddenly vanished from the face of the earth."[73] Most of the bones are found within a single 980-foot-long ravine in the Chinese countryside, about 415 miles southeast of Beijing. Clearly, processes were going on in the past that were so violent they are hardly imaginable.

10,000+ Duck-billed Dinosaurs Buried Alive in Montana

In his article titled, "The Extinction of the Dinosaurs," Creation researcher and career meteorologist Michael Oard describes some of the numerous dinosaur graveyards that are found all over the world.[74] He believes this is solid evidence of Noah's worldwide Flood. Oard reported that one of the largest bone beds in the world is located in north-central Montana:

> Based on outcrops, an extrapolated estimate was made for 10,000 duckbill dinosaurs entombed in a thin layer measuring 2 km east-west and 0.5 km north-south. The bones are disarticulated and disassociated, and are orientated east-west. However, a few bones were standing upright, indicating some type of debris flow. Moreover, there are no young juveniles or babies in this bone-bed, and the bones are all from one species of dinosaur.

Two other scientists, Horner and Gorman, also described the bone bed: "How could any mud slide, no matter how catastrophic, have the force to take a two- or three-ton animal that had just died and smash it around so much that its femur—

still embedded in the flesh of its thigh—split lengthwise?"[75] Oard concluded that a cataclysmic event is the best explanation for the arrangement of the bones.

Figure 26 shows the text from museum displays or articles about the particular dinosaur graveyard shown. Isn't it incredible that everyone admits that some type of watery catastrophe was responsible for piling up the dinosaurs into these mass graves?

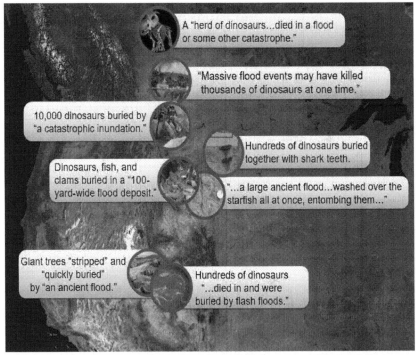

A "herd of dinosaurs...died in a flood or some other catastrophe."

"Massive flood events may have killed thousands of dinosaurs at one time."

10,000 dinosaurs buried by "a catastrophic inundation."

Hundreds of dinosaurs buried together with shark teeth.

Dinosaurs, fish, and clams buried in a "100-yard-wide flood deposit."

"...a large ancient flood...washed over the starfish all at once, entombing them..."

Giant trees "stripped" and "quickly buried" by "an ancient flood."

Hundreds of dinosaurs "...died in and were buried by flash floods."

Figure 26. Dinosaur Graveyards in Midwestern United States, with "Flood Catastrophe" Explanations Even from Secular Sources.[76]

Evidence #8: Dinosaur Fossils Are Frequently Mixed with Marine Fossils

Mainstream scientists who deny that dinosaurs were buried in the Global Flood seem to closely clutch a "trade secret"—that dinosaur fossils are commonly found with marine fossils.[77] This is especially true of the Hell Creek Formation in Montana, where five shark species and 14 species of fish fossils have been found alongside dinosaurs.[78]

What in the world are shark and fish doing with massive land dinosaurs? Did a tropical storm pick up the sharks and fish and bury them with the dinosaurs? It seems that the Flood provides just about the only logical explanation. The Bible states in Genesis 7:11: "In the six hundredth year of Noah's life, in the second month, the seventeenth day of the month, the same day were *all the fountains of the great deep broken up, and the windows of heaven were opened.*" This describes a catastrophe of incomprehensible proportions. Breaking up *all the fountains of the deep* describes a mechanism that could cause massive, worldwide tsunamis that could carry ocean water far onto the continents, especially if the fountains of the deep included magma, and that magma repaved and elevated the world's ocean floors as geophysicist John Baumgardner has modeled.[79]

In addition to the Hell Creek area, this "mixing" of marine and land creatures is also evident in the Dinosaur Provincial Park in Canada where 12 families of dinosaurs are found mixed together with fish, turtles, marsupials, and amphibians. In Morocco, they've discovered sharks, sawfish, ray-finned fishes, and coelocanths in the same rock layers as a Spinosaurus dinosaur.[80]

Evidence #9: Dinosaurs Are Frequently Buried without Juveniles

Jack Horner, secular paleontologist, has spent a lifetime in the field hunting dinosaur fossils. In his book, *Digging Dinosaurs*, Horner reported one of the oddest findings of his career: The discovery of a huge dinosaur graveyard—over 10,000 adult Maiasaura in a small area, and yet no young were mixed in with them.[81]

What could have caused this odd sorting? If one adopts the Biblical Creation view, the Flood provides a very practical explanation. As Dr. Tim Clarey explains: "The adult dinosaurs were likely stampeding away from the imminent danger of raging floodwaters; their young could not keep up and became engulfed in some lower part of the peninsula."[82] This would explain Horner's maiasaurs, as well as the age-sorted deposits described above.

Evidence #10: Fresh Dinosaur Biomaterials[83]

Next, we'll take a look at 14 short-lived dinosaur biomaterials that remain in dinosaur bones and other body parts like skin and horns. Decay experiments have placed outer limits on how long they should last before completely decaying. For each of these materials, their "expiration date" is well before 65 million years, which is when dinosaurs supposedly went extinct. So, rather than being 65 million years old, these materials are just thousands of years old. The science of protein decay fits the Bible's timeline of dinosaurs recently buried in Noah's Flood.

Secular scientists have published each of these dinosaur-era fresh biomaterials in peer-reviewed evolution-based science journals. One of most frequently used "rescuing devices" that's given by evolutionists to try to explain some of these findings is "bacterial contamination." However, microbes do not produce *any* of the biomaterials covered below, ruling out recent contamination.

For readers who would like to dive deeper into this line of research, we recommend the Spring 2015 issue of the *Creation Research Society Quarterly Journal*,[84] which includes a technical review of what's covered in summary form below.

Fresh Dinosaur Biomaterial #1: Blood Vessels

Blood vessels transport blood throughout the body. They include the tiny capillaries, through which water and chemicals pass between blood and the tissue. Bones include capillaries and larger vessels. Small, pancake-shaped cells loaded with long-lasting collagen protein comprise blood vessels.

The blood vessels shown in Figure 27 were discovered when Dr. Mary Schweitzer's team was attempting to move a gigantic *Tyrannosaurus rex* fossil by helicopter that turned out to be too heavy. They were forced to break apart the leg bone. When looking at the inside of the leg bone at the lab, they discovered that the inside of the bone was partially hollow (not mineralized), revealing the soft tissue shown in Figure 27 that was extracted after treatments to remove the minerals.[85]

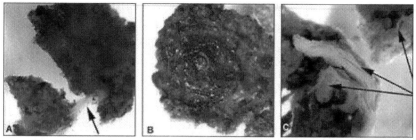

Figure 27. Tissue Fragments from a *Tyrannosaurus rex* Femur.[86]

The tissues that are shown on the left of Figure 27 show that it is flexible and resilient. When stretched, it returned to its original shape. The middle photo shows the bone after it was air dried. The photo at right shows regions of bone showing fibrous tissue, not normally seen in fossil bone.

Since this publication in 2005, blood vessels from several other dinosaurs and other extinct reptiles have been described and published in numerous leading scientific journals, including the *Annals of Anatomy*, *Science* (the leading journal of the American Association for the Advancement of Science), *Public Library of Sciences ONE*, and the *Proceedings from the Royal Society B*, which focuses on the biological sciences.[87]

Fresh Dinosaur Biomaterial #2: Red Blood Cells

Red blood cells carry oxygen and collect carbon dioxide using hemoglobin protein—also found in dinosaur and other fossils. Dr. Mary Schweitzer was one of the first to discover and publish the discovery of red blood cells, which she shares in her own words: "The lab filled with murmurs of amazement, for I had focused on something inside the vessels that none of us had ever noticed before: tiny round objects, translucent red with a dark center. Then a colleague took one look at them and shouted, 'You've got red blood cells. You've got red blood cells!'"[88]

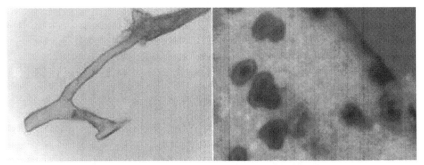

Figure 28. Red Blood Vessels and Cells from a *Tyrannosaurus rex* Bone.

These two photos in Figure 28 are from a 2005 discovery from Dr. Schweitzer that clearly show blood vessels from a *T. rex* bone (left) and red blood cells (right). How could these cells last for 65 million years? At least five peer-reviewed scientific journals have published accounts of red blood cells in dinosaur and other fossil bones.[89]

Regarding this discovery, Dr. Schweitzer remarked, "If you take a blood sample, and you stick it on a shelf, you have nothing recognizable in about a week. So why would there be anything left in dinosaurs?"[90] That's certainly a good question, and one that has an easier answer if dinosaurs are only thousands of years old!

After this discovery, Dr. Schweitzer ran into challenges when trying to publish her work in the scientific literature. Dr. Schweitzer remarks, "I had one reviewer tell me that he didn't care what the data said, he knew that what I was finding wasn't possible." Dr. Schweitzer wrote him back and asked, "Well, what type of data would convince you." The reviewer replied, "None."

Fresh Dinosaur Biomaterial #3: Hemoglobin

Hemoglobin protein contains iron and transports oxygen in red blood cells of most vertebrates. Some invertebrates, including certain insects and some worms, also use hemoglobin. In vertebrates, this amazing protein picks up oxygen from lungs or gills and carries it to the rest of the body's cells. There, oxygen fuels aerobic respiration by which cells produce energy.

Scientific studies have reported "striking evidence for the presence of hemoglobin derived peptides in the (T-rex) bone extract"[91] and several other dinosaur "era" bones.[92]

Fresh Dinosaur Biomaterial #4: Bone Cells (Osteocytes)

Secular scientists have described dinosaur proteins like hemoglobin, even though no experimental evidence supports the possibility that they can last for even a million years. But dinosaur bones hold more than just individual proteins. They sometimes retain whole cells and tissue remnants. An osteocyte is a bone cell that can live as long as the organism itself.

Osteocytes constantly rebuild bones and regulate bone mass. Figure 29 shows highly magnified blood vessels, blood products, and osteocytes that were found on the inside of a brow horn of a Triceratops.

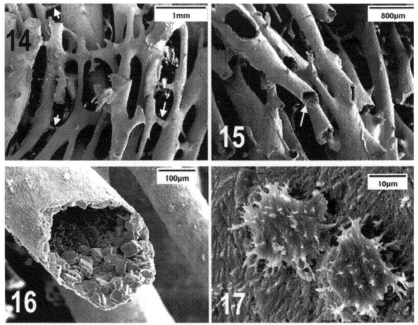

Figure 29. Soft Bone Material from a Brow Horn of a *Triceratops horridus* from Montana.[93]

Figure 29 shows blood vessels linked together (white arrows in frame 14). Frame 15 shows possible blood products lining inner wall of hardened vessel (white arrow). Frame 16 is enlarged from frame 15 and shows crystallized nature of possible blood products lining inner wall of hardened vessel. Frame 17 shows two large oblate osteocytes lying on fibrillar bone matrix.

At least four scientific studies have established osteocytes in dinosaur bones. One study even found nucleic acid signatures consistent with ancient DNA right where the nucleus would have been in dinosaur osteocytes.[94]

Fresh Dinosaur Biomaterial #5: Ovalbumin (Proteins)

Another protein found in fossils that microbes don't make is called ovalbumin. It makes up 60–65% of the total protein in egg whites. Ovalbumin has been found in exceptionally preserved sauropod eggs discovered in Patagonia, Argentina, a dig site that included skeletal remains and soft tissues of embryonic titanosaurid dinosaurs. These findings were reported in a peer-reviewed scientific journal.[95]

Fresh Dinosaur Biomaterial #6: Chitin

Chitin is a biochemical found in squid beaks and pens, arthropod exoskeletons, and certain fungi. If chitin was meant to last for millions of years, then it might have filled Earth's surface as dead insects, krill, and fungi left their remains over eons. Chitin is tough, but no known experiment supplies any reason to so much as suspect that it could last a million years, let alone hundreds of millions, as at least two scientific studies report finding in fossils.[96] Our Creator equipped many microbes with unique enzymes that digest chitin, so what could have kept those microbes away from all that chitin for millions of years?

Fresh Dinosaur Biomaterial #7: Unmineralized Bone

Fresh-looking, un-mineralized dinosaur bones pop up in dig sites around the world. In Alaska, for example, a petroleum geologist working for Shell Oil Company discovered well-preserved bones in Alaska along the Colville River. The bones looked so fresh that he assumed these were recently deposited, perhaps belonging to a mammoth or bison. Twenty years later scientists recognized them as Edmontosaurus bones—a duck-billed dinosaur.[97]

Figure 30. Unfossilized Hadrosaur Bone from the Liscomb Bone Bed.[98]

Mineralized bones can look darker than bone and typically feel quite heavy. Un-mineralized bones retain their original structure, often including the tiny pore spaces in spongy bone, as shown in Figure 30. One study includes an interesting section that states:

> Finally, a two-part mechanism, involving first cross-linking of molecular components and subsequent mineralization, is proposed to explain the surprising presence of still-soft elements in fossil bone. These results suggest that present models of fossilization processes may be incomplete and that *soft tissue elements may be more commonly preserved, even in older specimens, than previously thought.*[99]
> Additionally, in many cases, osteocytes with defined nuclei are preserved, and may represent

an important source for informative molecular data (emphasis added).

Numerous other studies published in scientific journals have described these un-mineralized dinosaur bone findings.[100] Sometimes evolutionists are surprised by the fact that many dinosaur bones contain "fresh," original bone. It seems that decades of conditioning that "dinosaur bones become solid rocks" and ideas of "millions of years" have framed assumptions that are frequently being broken today.

However, researchers out in the field—actually digging up bones—oftentimes have a different viewpoint. Take Dr. Mary Schweitzer's testimony for example, where she notes that many "fresh" dinosaur bones still have the stench of death:

> This shifting perspective clicked with Schweitzer's intuitions that dinosaur remains were more than chunks of stone. Once, when she was working with a *T. rex* skeleton harvested from Hell Creek, she noticed that the fossil exuded a distinctly organic odor. "It smelled just like one of the cadavers we had in the lab who had been treated with chemotherapy before he died," she says. Given the conventional wisdom that such fossils were made up entirely of minerals, Schweitzer was anxious when mentioning this to Horner [a leading paleontologist]. "But he said, 'Oh, yeah, all Hell Creek bones smell,'" she says. To most old-line paleontologists, the smell of death didn't even register. To Schweitzer, it meant that traces of life might still cling to those bones.[101]

Experienced dinosaur fossil collectors have developed similar opinions. Take experienced dinosaur hunter and wholesaler, Alan Stout, for example. Alan Stout is a long-time fossil collector and has collected and sold millions of dollars'

60

worth of dinosaur specimens to collectors, researchers, and museums worldwide.[102] After collecting in the Montana Hell Creek formation (and surrounding areas) for over a decade Alan states that many of the dinosaur bones he finds in the Cretaceous layers are only 40% mineralized, with as much as 60% of the bone being original material. He even notes that some of the fossils "look just like they were buried yesterday after scraping off just the outside layer of mineralization."[103]

Fresh Dinosaur Biomaterial #8: Collagen

Collagen is the main structural protein found in animal connective tissue. When boiled, collagen turns into gelatin, showing its sensitivity to temperature. In 2007, scientists discovered collagen amino acid sequences from a *T. rex* fossil that supposedly dated at 68 million years. Met with controversy, some suggested these proteins came from lab workers who accidentally contaminated the samples being studied. Or perhaps traces of ostrich bone proteins lingered in the equipment used in the study. Some even said, well perhaps "a bird died on top of the *T. rex* excavation site."[104] However, three separate labs verified collagen in dinosaurs in 2009[105] and again in January 2017.[106] The 2017 study even confirmed the collagen at the *molecular level*, and stated, "We are confident that the results we obtained are not contamination and that this collagen is original to the specimen."[107]

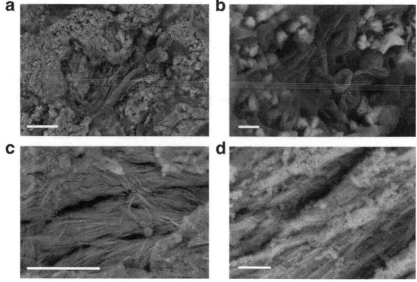

Figure 31. Fibers and Cellular Structures in Dinosaur Specimens.[108]

Experiments have projected that the absolute theoretical maximum life of collagen ranges from 300,000 to 900,000 years under the best possible conditions.[109] This shows that collagen proteins should not last one million years, but could (in the absence of microbes) last for thousands of years. This confronts millions-of-years age assignments for dinosaur remains, but is consistent with the biblical time frame.

But the "rescuing devices" being offered by evolutionists are not far behind. For example, in a recent article published in *Science*, Dr. Schweitzer tried to explain how the collagen sequences supposedly survived tens of millions of years: "… as red blood cells decay after an animal dies, iron liberated from their hemoglobin may react with nearby proteins, linking them together. This crosslinking, she says, causes proteins to precipitate out of solution, drying them out in a way that helps preserve them." Critical of this idea, however, Dr. Matthew Collins, a paleoproteomics expert at the University of York in the United Kingdom, stated that he doesn't think that the process described by Dr. Schweitzer could "arrest protein degradation for tens of millions of years, so he, for one, remains skeptical of Schweitzer's claim: 'Proteins decay in an orderly fashion. We can slow it down, but not by a lot.'"[110]

Fresh Dinosaur Biomaterial #9: DNA (Limited)

One measured decay rate of DNA, extracted from recently deposited fossil bird bones, showed a half-life of 521 years. DNA decays quickly. It should have spontaneously decayed into smaller chemicals after several tens of thousands of years—and it could only last that long if kept cool. A few brave secular scientists have reported DNA structures from dinosaur bones, although they did not directly address the question of its age.[111]

Fresh Dinosaur Biomaterial #10: Skin Pigments

In 2008, a group of paleontologists found exceptionally well-preserved Psittacosaurus remains in China and published images of dinosaur collagen fiber bundles. Other scientists published stunning skin color images from a separate Psittacosaurus, also from China, and found evidence of original, unaltered pigments including carotenoids and melanins. Nobody has performed an experiment that so much as suggests these pigments could last a million years. Still other studies have reported scale skin and hemoglobin decay products—still colored red as were some of Dr. Mary Schweitzer's *T. rex* and hadrosaurine samples—in a Kansas mosasaur.[112]

Fresh Dinosaur Biomaterial #11: PHEX (Proteins)

PHEX is a protein involved in bone mineralization in mammals. In 2013, Dr. Mary Schweitzer published detailed findings of the soft, transparent microstructures her team found in dinosaur bones. Because this discovery was so controversial, her team used advanced mass spectrometry techniques to sequence the collagen. Other methods demonstrated that proteins such as Actin, Tubulin, and PHEX found in osteocytes from two different dinosaurs were not from some form of contamination, but came from the creatures' remains.[113]

Fresh Dinosaur Biomaterial #12: Histone H4 (Proteins)

Bacteria do not make histone H4, but animals do. DNA wraps around it like a spool. Dr. Mary Schweitzer and her team found this protein inside a hadrosaur femur found in the Hell Creek Formation in Montana, which bears an assigned age of 67 million years. It might last for thousands of years if kept sterile, but no evidence so much as hints that it could last for a million years.[114]

Fresh Dinosaur Biomaterial #13: Keratin (Structural Protein)

Keratin forms the main structural constituent of hair, feathers, hoofs, claws, and horns. Some modern lizard skins contain tiny disks of keratin embedded in their scales. Researchers identified keratin protein in fossilized lizard skin scales from the Green River Formation that supposedly date to 50 million years ago. They explained its presence with a story about clay minerals attaching to the keratin to hold it in place for all that time. However, water would have to deposit the clay, and water helps rapidly degrade keratin. The most scientifically responsible explanation should be the simplest one—that this fossil is thousands, not millions of years old.[115] Other fossils with original keratin include Archaeopteryx[116] bird feather residue and stegosaur spikes.[117]

Fresh Dinosaur Biomaterial #14: Elastin

Elastin is a highly elastic protein found in connective tissue, skin, and bones. It helps body parts resume their shape after stretching or contracting, like when skin gets poked or pinched. Bacteria don't need it or make it, and elastin should not last a million years, even under the best preservation environment. Scientists reported finding this protein in a hadrosaur femur found in the Hell Creek Formation in Montana.[118]

Biomaterial Summary

Because these findings are game-changers, they are not without challenge by those who hold strongly to evolutionary ideas. Some of the "rescuing devices" that have been offered to attempt to explain these findings include iron in the blood acting as a preservative, the material being mistaken from a bird carcass mixed with the fossil, laboratory contamination, and even microbial biofilm (from bacteria in the bones). These explanations show an eagerness to attempt to dismiss the findings while clinging to the belief in millions of years. Rather than questioning the supposed long ages needed to prop up the evolutionary view, they seek other explanations to explain the presence of these materials.

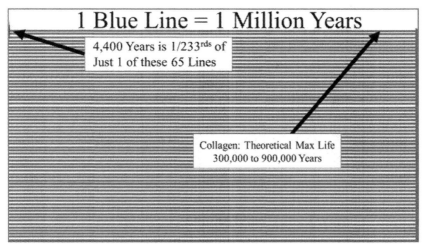

Figure 32. Dinosaur Biomaterials Time Comparison.

Figure 32 shows a simulated timeline to attempt to put these findings into perspective. Each of these 65 lines represents 1 million years. Showing 4,400 years on this chart is difficult, but is represented by a tiny dot in the upper left, which is 1/233rds of just one of these lines, or less than one-half of 1 percent of one of these lines. While this assumption can never be tested, some studies have measured an absolute theoretical maximum life of between 300,000 and 900,000 years.[119] If these dinosaur bones are really 65 million years old (and older), this collagen lasted for *72 to 217 times longer than these measured and extrapolated maximum collagen shelf lives.* Does this require strong faith?

Is it really possible that all 14 of these biomaterials lasted for 65 million years? If they represent more recent deposits and were quickly sealed in Noah's Flood only thousands of years ago, then these finds fit fine. The fact that these materials lasted even this long is remarkable, but within measured age estimates. These 14 fresh biomaterials—along with carbon-14 as we'll see next—clearly fit a timescale of just thousands of years more accurately than millions of years.

Evidence #11: Carbon-14 Found in Dinosaur Bones

Secular scientists typically don't look for carbon-14 in dinosaur bones because evolutionary deep time does not allow the possibility of recently-deposited dinosaurs. Carbon-14 decays so fast that all of it would spontaneously turn into nitrogen 14 in fewer than 100,000 years. According to evolutionists, why even look for it in samples that are supposed to be much older than this?

The Spring 2015 issue of the *Creation Research Society Quarterly Journal*[120] carried a study that tested seven dinosaur bones from Montana, Canada, and Oklahoma that five different laboratories detected carbon-14 in all samples from Cenozoic, Mesozoic, and Paleozoic source rocks. How did radiocarbon get there if it supposedly has a maximum shelf life of 100,000 years?

Several carbon-14 dating studies have shown the presence of carbon-14 in dinosaur bones and other fossils and Earth materials. If dinosaur bones are 100,000 years—let alone 65 million years—old, not one atom of carbon-14 should remain in them. But both secular and creation scientists have now published findings of small amounts of carbon-14 from ancient wood, coal, fish bones, lizard bones, ammonites, clams, diamonds, oil, marble, and dinosaur bone. It's as if the whole Earth's surface is thousands, not millions, of years old. But that means the Bible's history is correct and that evolutionary history leans more on imagination than observation.

Evidence #12: Dinosaur Mummies

Charles Sternberg discovered the first dinosaur mummy in Wyoming in 1908. This duck-billed dinosaur (*Edmontosaurus annectens*) was one of the finest dinosaur specimens discovered (until replaced by "Leonardo"—see below). It was the first dinosaur find on record that included a skeleton encased in skin impressions from large parts of the body (see Figure 33).

Figure 33. The Trachodon Mummy on Exhibit in the American Museum of Natural History (2008).[121]

CERTIFICATE

The best preserved dinosaur remains in the world belong to 'Leonardo', a 77 million-year-old Brachylophosaurus. Around 90% of the body is covered with fossilized soft tissue. It was discovered in 2000 in Montana, USA.

Keeper of the Records
GUINNESS WORLD RECORDS LTD

Dan Stephenson discovered "Leonardo" in 2000. This dinosaur mummy is one of the best-preserved dinosaur fossil in the world, which is about 90 percent covered in soft tissue, including skin, muscle, nail material, and a beak. Skin impressions have even been found on the underside of the skull and all along the neck, ribcage, legs, and left arm.[122] This finding was so well preserved it even made the *Guinness Book of World Records*!

Figure 34. Leonardo's Guinness World Record Certificate.

They even found the "fresh" content of Leonardo's last meal in his stomach! More than 40 different kinds of plants were found in his stomach and intestines, including tree leaves, flowers, ferns, shrubs and even algae that he likely swallowed getting a drink of water.[123] One must ask: How in the world did these soft tissues, leaves, flowers, and ferns last for over 77 million years? Seems very unlikely. Biblical creationists would place this animal about 4,400 years old, quickly buried by the Genesis Flood and sealed beneath sand for us to find today in "fresh" condition. Comparing the two worldviews, 77 million years is about *18,000 times longer* than 4,400 years.

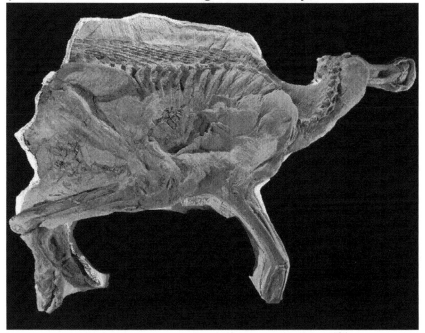

Figure 35. Leonardo Dinosaur Mummy.[124]

These types of finds do not surprise Biblical creationists. Rapidly-sealed animals can stay intact for thousands of years. But millions upon millions of years is another story!

Our discussion on collagen (above) provides some estimates on how soft tissues can possibly last thousands of years, but certainly not millions. Recently even a fossilized

69

heart was found that supposedly dates to over 113 million old.[125] A fossilized dinosaur brain was also recently discovered, dating to 133 million years old using the evolutionary timescale.[126]

Figure 36. Fossilized Dinosaur Brain.[127]

Soft tissues disintegrate. They go back to the dust. Seeing how some soft tissues can in fact be preserved and last for thousands of years testifies to both the *recent* and *catastrophic nature* of the Flood.

Conclusion

We've reviewed 12 lines of evidence that seem to align more with biblical history than evolution-based theories. We started with how dinosaurs seem to be "cleverly designed" with features that shout "intention" and "intelligent design."

Dinosaur fossil evidence shows that when these creatures are found in the crust of the earth, they always show up completely formed, with incredible design. Transitional forms that are "leading" to dinosaurs are simply not found. The evidence points to a magnificent designer placing the creatures here, fully-formed, and ready to live and thrive in a pre-Flood paradise.

The vast fossil record indicates catastrophic burial, with the animals furiously buried in mud—found fleeing in groups— and sometimes without juveniles. The fact that many dinosaur mass graves are found mixed together with marine fossils points to only one logical conclusion: the oceans came quickly onto dry land, burying both land- and sea-creatures simultaneously. Some dinosaurs are even buried so fast that they are mummified and found complete with their last meals still in their stomachs.

Finally, we have at least 14 "fresh" biomaterials found in dinosaur bones, horns, and claws that—according to even secular science—cannot last for millions of years. Finding detectable levels of carbon-14 in their bones also confirms a timescale of thousands of years, not millions.

Reading this book was not an academic exercise—these evidences beg a conclusion for each reader. If the biblical narrative is correct about dinosaurs, and we believe that it is, then it's also likely correct about *everything else*.[128] After diving into this research years ago, this is exactly what I learned. It became clear to me that the dinosaur data fit the biblical framework better than the evolutionary one, and it fueled my faith even more, solidifying my understanding that the Bible is true both theologically *and* historically.

Helpful Resources

The following websites are recommended for further research:

- Genesis Apologetics: *www.genesisapologetics.com*
- Debunking Evolution: *www.debunkevolution.com*
  Answers in Genesis: *www.answersingenesis.org*
- Answers in Genesis (High School Biology):
  www.evolutionexposed.com
- Creation Ministries International: *www.cmi.org*
- Creation Today: *www.creationtoday.org*
- Creation Wiki: *www.creationwiki.org*
- Evolution: The Grand Experiment with by Dr. Carl
  Werner: *www.thegrandexperiment.com*
- The Institute for Creation Research: *www.ICR.org*

Prayer of Salvation

You're not here by accident—God *loves* you and He *knows* who you are like no one else. His Word says:

Lord, You have searched me and known me. You know my sitting down and my rising up; you understand my thought afar off. You comprehend my path and my lying down, and are acquainted with all my ways. For there is not a word on my tongue, but behold, O Lord, You know it altogether. You have hedged me behind and before, and laid Your hand upon me. Such knowledge is too wonderful for me; It is high, I cannot attain it. (Psalm 139:1–6)

God loves you with an everlasting love, and with a love that can cover all of your transgressions—all that you have ever done wrong. But you have to repent of those sins and trust the Lord Jesus Christ for forgiveness. Your past is in the past. He wants to give you a new future and new hope.

But starting this new journey requires a step—a step of faith. God has already reached out to you as far as He can. By giving His son to die for your sins on the Cross, He's done everything He can to reach out to you. The next step is yours to take, and this step requires faith to receive His son into your heart. It also requires repentance (turning away) from your past sins–a surrendered heart that is willing to reject a sinful lifestyle. Many believers have a much easier time leaving sinful lifestyles after they fully trust Jesus and nobody else and nothing else. Along with forgiveness, the Holy Spirit enters your life when you receive Jesus, and He will lead you into a different lifestyle and way—a way that will lead to blessing, joy, patient endurance under trials, and eternal life.

If you are ready to receive Him, then you would recognize these key Biblical truths.[129]

1. Acknowledge that your sin separates you from God. The Bible describes sin in many ways. Most simply, sin is our failure to measure up to God's holiness and His righteous standards. We sin by things we do, choices we make, attitudes we show, and thoughts we entertain. We also sin when we fail to do right things or even think right thoughts. The Bible also says that all people are sinners: "there is none righteous, not even one." No matter how good we try to be, none of us does right things all the time. The Bible is clear, "For all have sinned and come short of the glory of God" (Romans 3:23).

2. Our sins demand punishment—the punishment of death and separation from God. However, because of His great love, God sent His only Son Jesus to die for our sins: "God demonstrates His own love for us in this: While we were still sinners, Christ died for us" (Romans 5:8). For you to come to God you have to get rid of your sin problem. But, in our own strength, not one of us can do this! You can't make yourself right with God by being a better person. Only God can rescue us from our sins. He is willing to do this not because of anything you can offer Him, but **just because He loves you**! "He saved us, not because of righteous things we had done, but because of His mercy" (Titus 3:5).

3. It's only God's grace that allows you to come to Him—not your efforts to "clean up your life" or work your way to Heaven. You can't earn it. It's a free gift: "For it is by grace you have been saved, through faith—and this not from yourselves, it is the gift of God—not by works, so that no one can boast" (Ephesians 2:8–9).

4. For you to come to God, the penalty for your sin must be paid. God's gift to you is His son, Jesus, who paid the debt for you when He died on the Cross. "For the wages of sin is death, but the gift of God is eternal life in Jesus Christ our Lord" (Romans 6:23). God brought Jesus

back from the dead. He provided the way for you to have a personal relationship with Him through Jesus.

When we realize how deeply our sin grieves the heart of God and how desperately we need a Savior, we are ready to receive God's offer of salvation. To admit we are sinners means turning away from our sin and selfishness and turning to follow Jesus. The Bible word for this is "repentance"—to change our thinking to acknowledge how grievous sin is, so our thinking is in line with God's.

All that's left for you to do is to accept the gift that Jesus is holding out for you right now: "If you confess with your mouth, 'Jesus is Lord,' and believe in your heart that God raised him from the dead, you will be saved. For it is with your heart that you believe and are justified, and it is with your mouth that you confess and are saved" (Romans 10:9–10). God says that if you believe in His son, Jesus, you can live forever with Him in glory: "For God so loved the world that He gave his one and only Son, that whoever believes in him shall not perish, but have eternal life" (John 3:16).

Are you ready to accept the gift of eternal life that Jesus is offering you right now? Let's review what this commitment involves:

- I acknowledge I am a sinner in need of a Savior. I repent or turn away from my sin.
- I believe in my heart that God raised Jesus from the dead. I trust that Jesus paid the full penalty for my sins.
- I confess Jesus as my Lord and my God. I surrender control of my life to Jesus.
- I receive Jesus as my Savior forever. I accept that God has done for me and in me what He promised.

If it is your sincere desire to receive Jesus into your heart as your personal Lord and Savior, then talk to God from your heart. Here's a suggested prayer:

*Lord Jesus, I know that I am a sinner and I do
not deserve eternal life. But, I believe You died
and rose from the grave to make me a new
creation and to prepare me to dwell in your
presence forever. Jesus, come into my life, take
control of my life, forgive my sins and save me. I
am now placing my trust in You alone for my
salvation and I accept your free gift of eternal
life.*

If you've prayed this prayer, it's important that you take these three next steps: First, go tell another Christian! Second, get plugged into a local church. Third, begin reading your Bible every day (we suggest starting with the book of John). Welcome to God's forever family!

Endnotes

[1] There are "dragon" legends in almost every culture in the world; ancient drawing and carvings of dinosaur-like creatures in almost every continent; and even several dragon/dinosaur accounts from several credible historians around the world—historians that are regarded as authorities in other areas, but whose accounts regarding dragons are dismissed by those holding to the older earth viewpoint. The reader is encouraged to draw from the resources at *www.answersingenesis.org* for books that discuss this area thoroughly.

[2] Image credit: *www.dinopedia.wikia.com* (January 26, 2017).

[3] While no expert really knows for sure how Triceratops' used their horns, many ideas have been proposed: Andrew A. Farke, 2004. "Horn Use in Triceratops (Dinosauria: Ceratopsidae): Testing Behavioral Hypotheses Using Scale Models." Palaeontologia Electronica 7(1):10, p. 3.

[4] J. Scannella and Jack Horner (2010) "Torosaurus Marsh, 1891 is Triceratops, Marsh, 1889 (Ceratopsidae: Chasmosaurinae) synonymy through ontogeny." *Journal of Vertebrate Paleontology* 30: 1157–1168.

[5] G.S. Paul and P. Christiansen, 2000. "Forelimb posture in neoceratopsian dinosaurs: Implications for gait and locomotion." *Paleobiology*, 26(3):450-465.

[6] Image credit: Wikipedia.

[7] Image credit: Shutterstock.

[8] Scannella & Horner (2010).

[9] An early reconstruction by Gregory S. Paul estimated Argentinosaurus at between 30–35 meters (98–115 ft.) in length and with a weight of up to 80–100 tonnes (88–110 short tons). The length of the skeletal restoration mounted in Museo Carmen Funes is 39.7 meters (130 ft.) long and 7.3 meters (24 ft.) high. This is the longest reconstruction in a museum and contains the original material, including a mostly complete fibula. Other estimates place the creature at 115 feet long and between 165,000 and 220,000 pounds (*www.bbc.co.uk/nature/life/Argentinosaurus*) (January 26, 2017).

[10] Image credit: Wikipedia.

[11] Carl Werner, *Living Fossils, Evolution: The Grand Experiment*, vol 1. (Green Forest, AR: New Leaf Press, 2009).

[12] "Fast Facts about the Bible." Bibleresources.org: *http://bibleresources.org/bibleresources/bible-facts/* (January 26, 2017)

[13] M. P. Taylor and M. J. Wedel. "Why sauropods had long necks; and why giraffes have short necks." *PeerJ* 1: (2013), e36.

[14] Image Credit: Wikipedia (*https://en.wikipedia.org/wiki/Mamenchisaurus*) (January 26, 2017).

[15] M.J. Wedel, "Aligerando a los gigantes (Lightening the giants)." *¡Fundamental!* 2007, 12:1–84. [in Spanish, with English translation]

[16] See also: "Mechanical implications of pneumatic neck vertebrae in sauropod dinosaurs." Daniela Schwarz-Wings, Christian A. Meyer, Eberhard Frey, Hans-Rudolf Manz-Steiner, Ralf Schumacher *Proc. R. Soc. B* 2010 277 11–17.

[17] Wedel, 2007.

[18] University of California Museum of Paleontology, Matt Wedel: Hunting the inflatable dinosaur *www.ucmp.berkeley.edu/science/profiles/wedel_0609.php* (January 26, 2017).

[19] Taylor & Wedel, 2013.

[20] Taylor & Wedel, 2013.

[21] Different types of sauropods had more or fewer vertebrae.

[22] David Catchpoole, Grass-eating dinos: A 'time-travel' problem for evolution (www.creation.com/grass-eating-dinos) (August 22, 2017); Brian Thomas, Dinosaurs Ate Rice, *www.icr.org/article/6428/* (August 22, 2017).

[23] Nicole Klein, Kristian Remes, Carole T. Gee, and P. Martin Sander, Biology of the Sauropod Dinosaurs Understanding the Life of Giants (Indiana University Press, 2011).

[24] M. Hallett & M. Wedel, *The Sauropod Dinosaurs: Life in the Age of Giants,* (Johns Hopkins University Press, 2016).

[25] Patrick Moser, Jordan River could die by 2011, Phys Org. *www.phys.org/news/2010-05-jordan-river-die.html* (May 2, 2010) (August 22, 2017).

[26] See, for example, the English Standard Version or the Life Application Study Bible notes.

[27] J. Carballido, D. Pol, A. Otero, I. Cerda, L. Salgado, A. Garrido, J. Ramezani, N. Cúneo, M. Krause, A new giant titanosaur sheds light on body mass evolution amongst sauropod dinosaurs, *Proceedings of the Royal Society B* (August 9, 2017).

[28] Nathan P. Myhrvold and Philip J. Currie, Supersonic Sauropods? Tail Dynamics in the Diplodocids, *Paleobiology* 23 (December, 1997): 393—409; Benjamin Meyers, W. Wayt Gibbs, Did a Dinosaur Break the Sound Barrier before We Did? (*www.scientificamerican.com/video/did-a-dinosaur-break-the-sound-barrier-before-we-did/*) (November 3, 2015) (August 22, 2017).

[29] Dattatreya Mandal, *Hexapolis*, Physical Model To Show How Dinosaurs May Have Whipped Their Tails In Supersonic Speed (October 16, 2015). (www.hexapolis.com/2015/10/16/physical-model-to-show-how-dinosaurs-may-have-whipped-their-tails-in-supersonic-speed/) (August 23, 2017).

[30] David Lambert, *The Encyclopedia of Dinosaurs* (London: Bloomsbury Books, 1994), p. 26–27, published in association with the British Museum of Natural History. Reconstructed graphic provided by Dr. Tommy Mitchell, Answers in Genesis.

78

[31] Carl Werner, *Evolution: The Grand Experiment* (3rd Edition). New Leaf Press. Kindle Edition. (Kindle Locations 1473-1476)

[32] Werner, p. 116

[33] Werner, Kindle Locations 2597-2599).

[34] Most Biblical creationists hold that some dinosaurs lived after the Flood, but the vast majority of these likely went extinct rather quickly for a multitude of reasons.

[35] Peter D. Ward, *Out of Thin Air: Dinosaurs, Birds, and Earth's Ancient Atmosphere*. (Washington, DC: Joseph Henry Press, 2006).

[36] See 2 Peter 3:6; Genesis 1; and Romans 8:22.

[37] See Romans 5:12 and 1 Corinthians 15:22.

[38] Dr. Andrew A. Snelling, "Noah's Lost World," 2014; last featured May 3, 2015 (*https://answersingenesis.org/geology/plate-tectonics/noahs-lost-world/*) (January 26, 2017).

[39] *The New Defender Study Bible* (Nashville, TN: World Publishing, 2006) states, "9:13 my bow. The rainbow, requiring small water droplets in the air, could not form in the pre-diluvian world, where the high vapor canopy precluded rain (Genesis 2:5). After the Flood, the very fact that rainfall is now possible makes a worldwide rainstorm impossible, and the rainbow "in the cloud" thereby becomes a perpetual reminder of God's grace, even in judgment." Several other Biblical Creation resources hold this view.

[40] Catherine Brahic, *New Scientist Daily News* (April 24, 2007). "Mystery prehistoric fossil verified as giant fungus": (*www.newscientist.com/article/dn11701-mystery-prehistoric-fossil-verified-as-giant-fungus/#.Uea7Qo2G18E*) (January 26, 2017).

[41] Image Credit: Shutterstock.

[42] It is commonly taught in evolution-based textbooks that the oxygen levels during the "Carboniferous" era were 35%. See, for example: David Beerling, *The emerald planet: how plants changed Earth's history*. (Oxford University Press, 2007), 47. Peter D. Ward, *Out of Thin Air: Dinosaurs, Birds, and Earth's Ancient Atmosphere*, (Washington, DC: Joseph Henry Press, 2006), Chapter 6. See also: R. A. Berner, D. J. Beerling, R. Dudley, J.M. Robinson, R.A Wildman, Jr. "Phanerozoic atmospheric oxygen." *Annual Review Earth Planet Science*, 2003, pp. 31, 105–134.

[43] Jeff Hecht, November 6, 1993, "Last gasp for the dinosaurs." *New Scientist*. *www.newscientist.com/article/mg14018981-200-last-gasp-for-the-dinosaurs/* (January 26, 2017).

[44] *The Washington Post*. "Lack of Oxygen Blamed for Dinosaurs' Extinction." October 28, 1993 *www.washingtonpost.com/archive/politics/1993/10/28/lack-of-oxygen-blamed-for-dinosaurs-extinction/84f102be-4264-4089-9e10-007b181476ee/?utm_term=.333d8cd2fefb* (January 26, 2017).

See also: R. A. Hengst, J. K. Rigby, G. P. Landis, R. L. Sloan. "Biological consequences of Mesozoic atmospheres: respiratory adaptations and functional range of Apatosaurus." In: Macleod N, Keller G, editors. *Cretaceous-Tertiary mass extinctions: biotic and environmental changes.* (New York: W.W. Norton & Co., 1996), pp. 327–347.

[45] Carl Wieland and Dr Jonathan Sarfati, "Some bugs do grow bigger with higher oxygen," *Journal of Creation* 25(1):13–14 (April 2011) (*http://creation.com/oxygen-bigger-bugs*) (January 26, 2017). See also J. Scheven, "The Carboniferous floating forest—an extinct pre-Flood ecosystem," *J. Creation* 10 (1):70–91, 1996.

[46] *Guinness World Book of Records 2014,* (The Jim Pattison Group, 2014), p. 27.

[47] Image Credit: Wikipedia.

[48] Gregory S. Paul, *Dinosaurs of the Air: The Evolution and Loss of Flight in Dinosaurs and Birds* (Johns Hopkins University Press, 2002), 472. See also: M.P. Witton and M.B. Habib. "On the Size and Flight Diversity of Giant Pterosaurs, the Use of Birds as Pterosaur Analogues and Comments on Pterosaur Flightlessness." *PLoS ONE*, 5(11) (2010). Other estimates place a range the weight range between 440 and 570 pounds: "That said, most mass estimates for the largest pterosaurs do converge, using multiple methods, around a 200–260kg [440–570lb] range at present, which represents decent confidence." (Ella Davies, BBC Earth, May 9, 2016) and "The biggest beast that ever flew had wings longer than a bus." (*www.bbc.com/earth/story/20160506-the-biggest-animals-that-ever-flew-are-long-extinct*) (January 26, 2017).

[49] Larry O' Hanlon, November 8, 2012. "This pterodactyl was so big it couldn't fly, scientist claims." *www.nbcnews.com/id/49746642/ns/technology_and_science-science/#.WH-U2_krKUn* (January 26, 2017).

[50] Mark P. Wilton, *Pterosaurs: Natural History, Evolution, Anatomy.* (Princeton University Press, 2013).

[51] Oxygen reported from within the amber bubbles are still debated among evolutionists.

[52] Ian Anderson, "Dinosaurs Breathed Air Rich in Oxygen," *New Scientist*, vol. 116, 1987, p. 25.

[53] Image Credit: Wikipedia.

[54] "No giants today: tracheal oxygen supply to the legs limits beetle size," was presented October 10-11 at Comparative Physiology 2006: Integrating Diversity (Virginia Beach). The research was carried out by Alexander Kaiser and Michael C. Quinlan of Midwestern University, Glendale, Arizona; J. Jake Socha and Wah-Keat Lee, Argonne National Laboratory, Argonne, IL; and Jaco Klok and Jon F. Harrison, Arizona State University, Tempe, AZ. Harrison is the principal investigator.

[55] Geological Society of America. "Raising giant insects to unravel ancient oxygen." *Science Daily*, October 30, 2010. *www.sciencedaily.com/releases/2010/10/101029132924.htm* (January 26, 2017). See also: Gauthier Chapelle & Lloyd S. Peck (May 1999). "Polar gigantism dictated by oxygen availability." *Nature*. 399 (6732): 114–115. This article argues that higher oxygen supply (30–35%) may also have led to larger insects during the Carboniferous period: A.N. Nel, G. Fleck, R. Garrouste, and G. Gand, "The Odonatoptera of the Late Permian Lodève Basin (Insecta)." *Journal of Iberian Geology* 34 (1) (2008): 115–122.

[56] Colin Schultz, "Long Before Trees Overtook the Land, Earth Was Covered by Giant Mushrooms," Smithsonian.com (July 17, 2013). *www.smithsonianmag.com/smart-news/long-before-trees-overtook-the-land-earth-was-covered-by-giant-mushrooms-13709647/* (January 26, 2017).

[57] University of Chicago News Office. "Prehistoric mystery organism verified as giant fungus 'Humongous fungus' towered over all life on land" *www-news.uchicago.edu/releases/07/070423.fungus.shtml* (April 23, 2007) (January 26, 2017).

[58] Simon J. Braddy, Markus Poschmann, and O. Erik Tetlie, "Giant claw reveals the largest ever arthropod," *Biological Letters*. (2008) 4 106–109 (Published February 23, 2008).

[59] M. G. Lockley & Christian Meyer. "The tradition of tracking dinosaurs in Europe," *Dinosaur Tracks and Other Fossil Footprints of Europe*. (Columbia University Press, 2013), pp. 25–52. See also: Donald R. Prothero, *Bringing Fossils to Life: An Introduction to Paleobiology*. Third Edition. (New York: Columbia University Press, 2015), p. 381.

[60] ThePaleobiology Database (Frequently Asked Questions): *https://paleobiodb.org/#/faq* (January 26, 2017)

[61] ThePaleobiology Database: *https://paleobiodb.org/navigator/* (January 26, 2017)

[62] RATE tested the assumptions using radiohalos and fission tracks. Both showed that the assumptions were violated (Larry Vardiman, Steven Austin, John Baumgardner, Steven Boyd, Eugene Chaffin, Donald DeYoung, D. Russell Humphreys, Andrew Snelling, *Radioisotopes and the Age of the Earth: Results of a Young-Earth Research Initiative*. The Institute for Creation Research).

[63] Ken Ham, "They Can't Allow 'It'!" AnswersinGenesis.org: *www.answersingenesis.org/articles/au/cant-allow-it* (January 1, 2014).

[64] Blake Edgar, "Dinosaur National Monument." *Dinosaur Digs*. (Bethesda, MD: Discovery Communications, 1999), p. 120.

[65] William A. Hoesch and Steven A. Austin, "Dinosaur National Monument: Jurassic Park Or Jurassic Jumble?" ICR.org: *www.icr.org/article/dinosaur-national-monument-park-or-jurassic-jumble/* (January 27, 2017).

[66] An articulated dinosaur skeleton means that a large number of the bones from an individual dinosaur were collected in close association, enough to reassemble the dinosaur.

[67] Werner, *Evolution: The Grand Experiment*, Kindle Locations 2598–2608).

[68] Other researchers have framed similar explanations about the same area: "It looks like catastrophe… We think a herd was trying to cross a river in flood. These animals weren't too bright." Phillip Currie, quoted in Rick Gore, "Dinosaurs." *National Geographic*, January 1993, p. 46.

[69] Werner, *Evolution: The Grand Experiment* (Kindle Locations 2598–2608).

[70] There is disagreement in the paleontology field as to whether the "dinosaur death pose" is due to choking while dying from drowning, or due to strong water currents arching the neck back after death. See: Achim G. Reisdorf & Michael Wuttke, "Re-evaluating Moodie's Opisthotonic-Posture Hypothesis in Fossil Vertebrates Part I: Reptiles—the taphonomy of the bipedal dinosaurs Compsognathus longipes and Juravenator starki from the Solnhofen Archipelago (Jurassic, Germany)," *Palaeobiodiversity and Palaeoenvironments* 92 (2012):119–168. Their findings stated, "From what has been presented above, it can be concluded that the formation of the 'opisthotonic posture' in *subaquatically deposited carcasses* of long-necked and long tailed reptiles is the result of a postmortem process…this posture must be seen as a normal phenomenon that occurs during subaquatic gradual embedding of these sorts of carcasses." See discussion: Drwile.com, "Arched Necks in Dinosaur Fossils: Is Water to Blame?" *www.blog.drwile.com/?p=7118* (February 16, 2016).

[71] D.A. Eberth, D.B. Brinkman, and V.A. Barkas, "Centrosaurine Mega-bonebed from the Upper Cretaceous of Southern Alberta: Implications for Behaviour and Death Events" in *New Perspectives on Horned Dinosaurs: The Ceratopsian Symposium at the Royal Tyrrell Museum* (September 2007).

[72] *New Perspectives on Horned Dinosaurs: The Ceratopsian Symposium at the Royal Tyrrell Museum* (September 2007).

[73] Michael Reilly, "Dinosaurs' Last Stand Found in China?" Discovery.com: *www.news.discovery.com/earth/dinosaurs-last-stand-found-in-china.htm* (January 1, 2014).

[74] Michael J. Oard, "The Extinction of the Dinosaurs," *Journal of Creation* 11(2) (1997): 137–154.

[75] J.R. Horner & J. Gorman, *Digging Dinosaurs*. New York: Workman Publishing, 1988, pp. 122–123.

[76] Credit: Caleb LePore. See: David Maxwell Braun, "Dinosaur Herd Found in Canada Named After Science Teacher." *National Geographic News*. National Geographic Society, October 2, 2008; Christopher A. Brochu, M. K. Brett-Surman. "Dinosaur Provincial Park." *A Guide to Dinosaurs*. (San Francisco, CA: Fog City, 2002), p. 220; John R. Horner and James Gorman. *Digging Dinosaurs*. (New York: Workman Pub., 1988), p. 131; Brett French,

"New Finds, Old Site: Dinosaur Dig Revealing Insights into Montana 103 Million Years Ago." *Butte Montana Local News.* (August 23, 2015); Brett French, "Jurassic Starfish Discovery in South-central Montana Wows Researchers." *Independent Record.* (July 6, 2015); Blake Edgar, "Petrified Forest National Park." *Dinosaur Digs.* (Bethesda, MD: Discovery Communications, 1999), p. 104; Glendive Dinosaur and Fossil Museum, Glendive, Montana; Mike Dunham, "Scientists Identify Dinosaur That Roamed the Alaska Arctic." *Alaska Dispatch News.* Alaska Dispatch Publishing. (September 22, 2015).

[77] Tim Clarey, Ph.D. "Dinosaurs in Marine Sediments: A Worldwide Phenomenon." *Acts & Facts.* 44 (6) (2015).

[78] J. H. Hartman and J. I. Kirkland. "Brackish and marine mollusks of the Hell Creek Formation of North Dakota: Evidence for a persisting Cretaceous seaway." In *The Hell Creek Formation and the Cretaceous-Tertiary Boundary in the Northern Great Plains: An Integrated Continental Record of the End of the Cretaceous.* J. H. Hartman, K. R. Johnson, and D. J. Nichols, eds. Geological Society of America Special Paper 361, pp. 271–296. (2002); W. A. Clemens and J. H. Hartman. "From Tyrannosaurus rex to asteroid impact: Early studies (1901–1980) of the Hell Creek Formation in its type area." In *Through the End of the Cretaceous in the Type Locality of the Hell Creek Formation in Montana and Adjacent Areas.* Wilson, G. P. et al, eds. Geological Society of America Special Paper 503, pp. 1–87. 2014.

[79] Jesse A. Sherburn, John R. Baumgardner and Mark F. Horstemeyer, "New Material Model Reveals Inherent Tendency in Mantle Minerals for Runaway Mantle Dynamics," *International Conference on Creationism* (2013).

[80] N. Ibrahim, et al. 2014. "Semiaquatic adaptations in a giant predatory dinosaur." *Science.* 345 (6204): 1613–1616.

[81] Horner & Gorman, *Digging Dinosaurs,* 128.

[82] Tim Clarey, Ph.D. "Dinosaurs in Marine Sediments: A Worldwide Phenomenon." *Acts & Facts.* 44 (6) (2015).

[83] I am grateful for the review and input on this section from Brian Thomas and Pat Roy.

[84] *Creation Research Society Quarterly Journal* Spring 2015 (Volume 51, Number 4): *www.creationresearch.org/index.php/component/k2/item/118-2015-volume-51-number-4-spring* (January 27, 2017)

[85] Jeff Hecht, Daily News, "Blood vessels recovered from T. rex bone," NewScientist.com: *www.newscientist.com/article/dn7195-blood-vessels-recovered-from-t-rex-bone/* (March 24, 2005)

[86] Science via AP (*www.msnbc.msn.com/id/7285683/*) (January 27, 2017).

[87] See, for example: R. Pawlicki and M. Wowogrodzka-Zagorska. "Blood vessels and red blood cells preserved in dinosaur bones." Annals of Anatomy 180 (1998): 73–77; M. H. Schweitzer, J.L. Wittmeyer, J.R. Horner, and J.K Toporske. "Soft-tissue vessels and cellular preservation in Tyrannosaurus rex." *Science,* 307 (2005): 1952; M.H. Schweitzer, J.L. Wittmeyer, and J.R. Horner. "Soft tissue and cellular preservation in vertebrate skeletal elements from the Cretaceous to the present." *Proceedings of the Royal Society B* 274 (2007): 183–197; M.H. Schweitzer, W. Zheng, C.L. Organ, R. Avci, Z. Suo, L.M. Freimark, V.S. Lebleu, M.B. Duncan, M.G. Vander Heiden, J.M. Neveu, W.S. Lane, J.S. Cottrell, J.R. Horner, L.C. Cantley, R. Kalluri, and J.M. Asara. "Biomolecular characterization and protein sequences of the campanian Hadrosaur B. Canadensis." *Science,* 324 (2009): 626–631.

[88] M. Schweitzer and I. Staedter, *The Real Jurassic Park, Earth,* June 1997, pp. 55–57.

[89] R. Pawlicki and M. Wowogrodzka-Zagorska. "Blood vessels and red blood cells preserved in dinosaur bones." *Annals of Anatomy* 180 (1998): 73–77; M. H. Schweitzer, J.L. Wittmeyer, J.R. Horner, and J.K Toporske. "Soft-tissue vessels and cellular preservation in Tyrannosaurus rex." *Science,* 307 (2005): 1952; M.H. Schweitzer, J.L. Wittmeyer, and J.R. Horner. "Soft tissue and cellular preservation in vertebrate skeletal elements from the Cretaceous to the present." *Proceedings of the Royal Society B* 274 (2007): 183–197; M.H. Schweitzer, W. Zheng, C.L. Organ, R. Avci, Z. Suo, L.M. Freimark, V.S. Lebleu, M.B. Duncan, M.G. Vander Heiden, J.M. Neveu, W.S. Lane, J.S. Cottrell, J.R. Horner, L.C. Cantley, R. Kalluri, and J.M. Asara. "Biomolecular characterization and protein sequences of the campanian Hadrosaur B. Canadensis." *Science* 324 (2009): 626–631; J. Lindgren, M.W. Caldwell, T. Konishi, L.M. Chiappe, "Convergent Evolution in Aquatic Tetrapods: Insights from an Exceptional Fossil Mosasaur." *PLoS ONE* 5(8) (2010): e11998.

[90] Barry Yeoman, "Schweitzer's Dangerous Discovery," Discovery Magazine: www.discovermagazine.com/2006/apr/dinosaur-dna (April 27, 2006) (January 27, 2017).

[91] M.H. Schweitzer, M. Marhsall, K. Carron, D.S. Bohle, S.C. Busse, E.V. Arnold, D. Barnard, J.R. Horner, and J.R. Starkey. "Heme compounds in dinosaur trabecular bone." *Proceedings of the National Academy of Sciences* USA 94, (1997), p. 6295.

[92] J.M. Asara, M.H. Schweitzer, L.M. Freimark, M. Phillips, and L.C. Cantley. "Protein sequences from mastodon and Tyrannosaurus rex revealed by mass spectrometry." *Science,* 316 (2007): 280–285.

[93] M. Armitage, "Soft bone material from a brow horn of a Triceratops horridus from Hell Creek Formation, MT." *Creation Research Society Quarterly,* 51 (2015): 248–258.

[94] M.H. Schweitzer, W. Zheng, T.P. Cleland, and M. Bern. "Molecular analyses of dinosaur osteocytes support the presence of endogenous molecules." *Bone,* 52 (2013): 414–423; M. Armitage, "Soft bone material from a brow horn of a Triceratops horridus from Hell Creek Formation, MT." *Creation Research Society Quarterly,* 51 (2015): 248–258; M. Armitage and K.L. Anderson. "Soft tissue of fibrillar bone from a fossil of the supraorbital horn of the dinosaur Triceratops horridus." *Acta Histochemica,* 115 (2013):603–608; R. Pawlicki, "Histochemical demonstration of DNA in osteocytes from dinosaur bones." *Folia Histochemica Et Cytobiologica,* 33 (1995): 183–186.

[95] M.H. Schweitzer, et al. 2005. "Molecular preservation in Late Cretaceous sauropod dinosaur eggshells." *Proceedings of the Royal Society B: Biological Sciences.* 272 (1565): 775–784.

[96] G.D. Cody, N.S. Gupta, D.E.G. Briggs, A.L.D. Kilcoyne, R.E. Summons, F. Kenig, R.E. Plotnick, and A. C. Scott. "Molecular signature of chitin-protein complex in Paleozoic arthropods." *Geology,* 39 (3) (2011): 255–258; H. Ehrlich, J.K. Rigby, J.P. Botting, M.V. Tsurkan, C. Werner, P. Schwille, Z. Petrášek, A. Pisera, P. Simon, V.N. Sivkov, D.V. Vyalikh, S.L. Molodtsov, D. Kurek, M. Kammer, S. Hunoldt, R. Born, D. Stawski, A. Steinhof, V.V. Bazhenov, and T. Geisler. "Discovery of 505-million-year old chitin in the basal demosponge Vauxia gracilenta." *Scientific Reports.* 3 (2013): 3497.

[97] M. Helder, "Fresh dinosaur bones found," *Creation* 14(3) (1992): 16–17, *www.creation.com/fresh-dinosaur-bones-found* (January 27, 2017).

[98] "Fossils of new duck-billed, plant-eating dinosaur species found in Alaska, researchers say" (*www:accesswdun.com/article/2015/9/337248)* (September 22, 2015).

[99] M.H. Schweitzer, J.L. Wittmeyer, and J.R. Horner. "Soft tissue and cellular preservation in vertebrate skeletal elements from the Cretaceous to the present." *Proceedings of the Royal Society B,* 274 (2007):183–197.

[100] Hirotsugu Mori, Patrick S. Druckenmiller, and Gregory M. Erickson, "A new Arctic hadrosaurid from the Prince Creek Formation (lower Maastrichtian) of northern Alaska." *Acta Palaeontologica Polonica* 61 (1), (2016): 15–32; A.R. Fiorillo, P.J. McCarthy, and P.P. Flaig "Taphonomic and sedimentologic interpretations of the dinosaur-bearing Upper Cretaceous Strata of the Prince Creek Formation, Northern Alaska: Insights from an ancient high-latitude terrestrial ecosystem." *Palaeogeography, Palaeoclimatology, Palaeoecology* 295 (2010): 376–388; R.A. Gangloff and A.R. Fiorillo, "Taphonomy and paleoecology of a bonebed from the Prince Creek Formation, North Slope, Alaska." *Palaios,* 25 (2010): 299–317; M.H. Schweitzer, C. Johnson, T.G. Zocco, J.R. Horner, and J.R. Starkey, "Preservation of biomolecules in cancellous bone of Tyrannosaurus rex," *J. Vertebrate paleontology* 17 (2) (1997): 349–359;

M.H. Schweitzer, M. Marshall, K. Carron, D.S. Bohle, S.C. Busse, E.V. Arnold, D. Barnard, J.R. Horner, and J.R. Starkey, "Heme compounds in dinosaur trabecular bone," *Proceedings of the National Academy of Science* 94 (1997): 6291–6296; As stated in Helder (above): "An initial announcement was printed in 1985 in Geological Society of America abstract programs Vol.17, p. 548. Already in press at that time was an article describing the site and the condition of the bones (Kyle L. Davies, 'Duck-bill Dinosaurs (Hadrosauridae, Ornithischia) from the North Slope of Alaska', Journal of Paleontology, Vol.61 No.1, pp.198-200); M.H. Schweitzer, J.L. Wittmeyer, and J.R. Horner. "Soft tissue and cellular preservation in vertebrate skeletal elements from the Cretaceous to the present." *Proceedings of the Royal Society B,* 274 (2007): 183–197.

[101] Barry Yeoman, "Schweitzer's Dangerous Discovery," Discovery Magazine: *www.discovermagazine.com/2006/apr/dinosaur-dna* (April 27, 2006) (January 27, 2017).

[102] Severo Avila, "Alan Stout is the Bone Collector," Northwest Georgia News: *www.northwestgeorgianews.com/rome/lifestyles/alan-stout-is-the-bone-collector/article_6b1268e7-3350-5dfd-a3dc-652dcf27d174.html* (April 11, 2010) (January 27, 2017).

[103] Alan Stout, Personal communication, January 16, 2017.

[104] Marshall Bern, Brett S. Phinney, and David Goldberg. "Reanalysis of Tyrannosaurus Rex Mass Spectra." *Journal of Proteome Research* 8.9 (2009): 4328–4332.

[105] Brian Thomas, "Original Biomaterials in Fossils." *Creation Research Society Quarterly*, 51 (2015): 234–347.

[106] Elena R. Schroeter, Caroline J. DeHart, Timothy P. Cleland, Wenxia Zheng, Paul M. Thomas, Neil L. Kelleher, Marshall Bern, and Mary H. Schweitzer, "Expansion for the Brachylophosaurus canadensis Collagen I Sequence and Additional Evidence of the Preservation of Cretaceous Protein." Journal of Proteome Research Article.

[107] See UPI News: *www.upi.com/Science_News/2017/01/23/Scientists-find-ancient-dinosaur-collagen/6091485202598/* (January 23, 2017).

[108] S. Bertazzo, et al. "Fibres and cellular structures preserved in 75-million-year-old dinosaur specimens," *Nature Communications*, 6, (2015).

[109] M. Buckley and M.J. Collins. "Collagen survival and its use for species identification in Holocene-Lower Pleistocene bone fragments from British archaeological and paleontological sites." *Antiqua*, 1 (2011): e1.

[110] Robert F. Service, "Scientists retrieve 80-million-year-old dinosaur protein in 'milestone' paper," Science.com: *www.sciencemag.org/news/2017/01/scientists-retrieve-80-million-year-old-dinosaur-protein-milestone-paper* (January 31, 2017) (February 5, 2017).

[111] M. H. Schweitzer, et al. "Molecular analyses of dinosaur osteocytes support the presence of endogenous molecules." *Bone*, 52 (1) (2013): 414–423. S. R. Woodward, N. J. Weyand, and M. Bunnell. "DNA Sequence from Cretaceous Period Bone Fragments." *Science*, 266 (5188) (1994): 1229–1232.

[112] T. Lingham-Soliar, "A unique cross section through the skin of the dinosaur Psittacosaurus from China showing a complex fibre architecture." *Proceedings of the Royal Society B: Biological Sciences* 275 (2008): 775–780. T. Lingham-Soliar and G. Plodowski. "The integument of Psittacosaurus from Liaoning Province, China: taphonomy, epidermal patterns and color of a ceratopsian dinosaur." *Naturwissenschaften* 97 (2010): 479–486.

[113] M.H. Schweitzer, W. Zheng, T.P. Cleland, and M. Bern. Molecular analyses of dinosaur osteocytes support the presence of endogenous molecules. *Bone,* 52 (2013): 414–423.

[114] Ibid.

[115] N.P. Edwards, H.E. Barden, B.E. van Dongen, P.L. Manning, P.O. Larson, U. Bergmann, W.I. Sellers, and R.A. Wogelius. "Infrared mapping resolves soft tissue preservation in 50 million year-old reptile skin." *Proceedings of the Royal Society B,* 278 (2011): 3209–3218.

[116] U. Bergmann, et al., "Archaeopteryx feathers and bone chemistry fully revealed via synchrotron imaging." *Proceedings of the National Academy of Sciences.* 107 (20) (2010), 9060–9065.

[117] S. Hayashi, K. Carpenter, M. Watabe, and L.A. McWhinney, "Ontogenetic histology of Stegosaurus plates and spikes." *Palaeontology* 55 (2012), 145–161.

[118] M.H. Schweitzer, W. Zheng, C.L. Organ, R. Avci, Z. Suo, L.M. Freimark, V.S. Lebleu, M.B. Duncan, M.G. Vander Heiden, J.M. Neveu, W.S. Lane, J.S. Cottrell, J.R. Horner, L.C. Cantley, R. Kalluri, and J.M. Asara. "Biomolecular characterization and protein sequences of the campanian Hadrosaur B. Canadensis." *Science,* 324 (2009): 626–631.

[119] M. Buckley and M.J. Collins. "Collagen survival and its use for species identification in Holocene-Lower Pleistocene bone fragments from British archaeological and paleontological sites." *Antiqua,* 1 (2011): e1. Hypothetically, if dinosaurs include an unrealistically large mass of initial collagen, it may last as long as 1.7 million years (see Brian Thomas, "A Review of Original Tissue Fossils and their Age Implications," Proceedings of the Seventh International Conference on Creationism [Pittsburgh, PA: Creation Science Fellowship]). However, this upper estimate assumes that skin, muscles, and connective tissue collagen decays as slowly as bone collagen, which is not typically the case (Brian Thomas, personal communication, February 15, 2017).

[120] *Creation Research Society Quarterly Journal,* Spring 2015 (Volume 51, Number 4): *www.creationresearch.org/index.php/component/k2/item/118-2015-volume-51-number-4-spring* (January 27, 2017).

[121] Image Credit: Wikipedia: *www.commons.wikimedia.org/wiki/File:Edmontosaurus_mummy.jpg*

[122] Image Credit: Wikipedia: *www.news.nationalgeographic.com/news/2002/10/1010_021010_dinomummy.html*

[123] Image Credit: Dinosaur Mummy: *www.dinosaurmummy.org/guide-to-dinosaur-mummy-csi.html*

[124] Image Credit: Wikipedia: https://upload.wikimedia.org/wikipedia/commons/thumb/2/28/Leonardo_mummified_brachylophosaurus.jpg/1280px-Leonardo_mummified_brachylophosaurus.jpg

[125] Michael Greshko, "Hearts of Stone: A Fabulous Fossil Find," National Geographic: *http://news.nationalgeographic.com/2016/04/160421-fossils-hearts-fish-evolution-paleontology-science/* (April 21, 2016) (January 27, 2017).

[126] Nicholas St. Fleur, "First Fossilized Dinosaur Brain Found." New York Times: *www.nytimes.com/2016/10/28/science/first-fossilized-dinosaur-brain.html?_r=0* (October 27, 2016) (January 27, 2017).

[127] Image Credit: *www.ox.ac.uk/news/2016-10-28-fossilised-dinosaur-brain-tissue-identified-first-time* (January 27, 2017)

[128] The author pre-supposes the truth and accuracy of Scripture.

[129] Summarized from: Southern Baptist Convention. "How to Become a Christian." *www.sbc.net/knowjesus/theplan.asp.* Accessed March 16, 2016.

Made in the USA
San Bernardino, CA
28 August 2017